Commercial Property Conversion Mastery

All You Need to Know in Property Investment

By Obinna Okeke

ISBN:9798249979850

Preface

The landscape of property investment in the United Kingdom has changed more in the last decade than in the previous fifty years. High streets have evolved, office demand has shifted, and entire sectors of commercial real estate have been reshaped by technology, remote work, and changing consumer behavior. At the same time, the demand for quality housing has continued to rise creating one of the most significant structural opportunities in modern property investment: commercial-to-residential conversion. This book was born from that shift.

For years, investors focused almost exclusively on traditional buy-to-let, HMOs, and small refurbishments. But as planning rules evolved, particularly with the introduction of Class MA, a new path opened one that rewards creativity, strategic thinking, and the ability to see potential where others see decline. Commercial conversion is not simply a niche strategy; it is a response to a national need. It transforms empty buildings into homes, revitalizes communities, and creates long-term value for those who understand how to navigate its complexities.

Yet despite its potential, commercial conversion remains misunderstood. Many investors assume it is too complicated, too expensive, or too risky. Others believe it is reserved for large developers with deep pockets and decades of experience. The truth is far more empowering: with the right knowledge, the right team, and the right approach, commercial conversion is accessible, achievable, and scalable even for those starting with modest resources.

This book is designed to bridge that gap.

It distils the entire process sourcing, analyzing, planning, financing, converting, and exiting into a clear, structured roadmap. It removes the mystery from planning policy, demystifies development finance, and breaks down the technical aspects of construction into practical, actionable steps. It also highlights the risks, the pitfalls, and the realities of working with older commercial buildings, because success

in this field requires both ambition and discipline.
Whether you are reading this as a complete beginner or an experienced investor looking to expand your strategy, my goal is simple: to give you the clarity, confidence, and competence to take your first step into commercial conversion and to keep going.
The buildings are waiting.
The opportunity is real.

Obinna

Dedication

To every dreamer who has walked past an empty building and imagined something better.

To the creators, the builders, the problem-solvers, the ones who believe that forgotten spaces can become homes, and that regeneration begins with vision.

And to my family, whose support, patience, and belief make every chapter possible

Acknowledgements

This book is the result of years of learning, refining, and collaborating with people who have shaped my understanding of commercial property and the power of transformation.

To the architects, planners, surveyors, and contractors who generously shared their expertise thank you for expanding my perspective and challenging my assumptions.

To the investors and developers who trusted me with their stories, insights, and lessons your experiences helped shape the real-world examples in these pages.

To my readers, students, and community, your hunger for knowledge and your courage to take action inspire me every day. You are the reason this book exists.

And finally, to everyone who believes in the potential of commercial conversion to create homes, strengthen communities, and build long-term wealth, this work is for you.

Obinna

Table of Contents

Introduction: The UK Landscape & Future Outlook

The UK Property Market at a Historic Crossroads

The UK property market is standing at one of the most significant turning points in its modern history. For decades, the rhythm of British life revolved around the high street and the office corridor. These spaces were more than just buildings; they were the backbone of local economies, the anchors of community identity, and the primary destinations for work, shopping, and social interaction. Yet as we move deeper into 2026, it has become clear that the traditional commercial landscape has shifted permanently. The forces reshaping the country are not temporary fluctuations but structural changes that have altered how people live, work, and use space.

On paper, the national economy appears steady, with GDP growth hovering at modest but stable levels. But the real story is not found in the headline numbers. It is found in the quiet transformation happening in towns and cities across the country. Remote work has become a permanent fixture of professional life, reducing the daily demand for office space. Online shopping continues to dominate consumer behavior, leaving many retail units empty or underused. Banks, travel agencies, and service providers that once required a physical presence have migrated online, leaving behind a trail of vacant commercial properties that no longer serve their original purpose.

At the same time, the UK faces a deep and persistent housing shortage. Demand for residential accommodation has never been higher, driven by population growth, urbanization, and the rising expectations of younger generations seeking flexible, modern living spaces. Local councils are under immense pressure to deliver more homes, yet they often lack the land, funding, or political appetite to approve large-scale new developments. The result is a widening gap between the number of homes needed and the number being built.

This is the crossroads: a surplus of commercial space on one side, and a desperate need for residential housing on the other. The government has recognized this imbalance and responded with one of the most impactful planning reforms in decades. The introduction of the "Class E" designation and the expansion of Permitted Development Rights (PDR) have fundamentally changed the rules of engagement. These reforms signal a clear message: the future of development lies not in expanding outward, but in transforming what already exists. Instead of relying solely on new construction, the government is encouraging investors and developers to reimagine the buildings that have been left behind by economic and technological change.

This shift has created a unique moment of opportunity. Commercial properties that once depended on footfall, retail demand, or office occupancy are now being viewed through a new lens. They are no longer seen as relics of a declining commercial era, but as raw material for residential living. This is where commercial property conversion emerges as a powerful strategy, a strategy that sits at the intersection of planning reform, housing need, and investor potential. It is a strategy built on creativity, adaptability, and the ability to see value where others see decline.

Commercial conversion is not simply a response to market conditions; it is a redefinition of how we use space in the twenty-first century. And for those who understand it, this moment represents not just an opportunity, but a generational shift in the way wealth can be built through property. From an investor's perspective, commercial conversion offers three powerful defensive advantages:

Wedge Against Inflation

One of the most compelling reasons commercial property conversions has surged in popularity is its natural ability to protect investors from the silent erosion of wealth caused by inflation. Inflation is not dramatic. It doesn't arrive with alarms or headlines. It creeps in quietly, month after month, reducing the purchasing power of money and weakening the value of savings held in cash. For many people, inflation feels abstract a number announced by economists or debated on television. But for property investors, inflation is a very real force that shapes return, influences strategy, and determines long-term financial resilience.

Property, unlike cash, is a tangible asset. It exists in the physical world. It cannot be printed, diluted, or devalued by government policy in the same way currency can. When inflation rises, the cost of living rises with it and so do the costs of building materials, labor, and new construction. This makes existing properties more valuable by comparison. A building you convert today becomes more expensive to replicate tomorrow. In this way, property naturally appreciates over time, not because of speculation, but because the cost of replacing it increases year after year.

Residential rents also tend to move in line with inflation. As the cost of goods and services rises, so does the cost of housing. Tenants expect annual rent adjustments, and the market absorbs these increases because housing is not optional. People may cut back on travel, entertainment, or luxury purchases during inflationary periods, but they cannot cut back on shelter. This creates a built-in mechanism that allows landlords to maintain and often grow their income even as the value of money declines.

Commercial conversions amplify this protective effect. When you take a commercial building and transform it into residential units, you are not simply buying an asset; you are creating one. You are adding value through design, planning, and construction. This value is not tied to inflation in the same way cash is. Instead, it is tied to the demand for housing, which remains strong regardless of economic cycles. Even during periods of high inflation, people still need places to live, and the pressure on the housing market often intensifies as new construction becomes more expensive and slower to deliver.

Furthermore, commercial conversions allow investors to lock in long-term financing at fixed rates, while rental income continues to rise with inflation. This creates a widening gap between stable debt payments and increasing revenue a powerful wealth-building dynamic that protects investors from economic volatility. Over time, inflation effectively pays down the real value of the debt, while the property itself grows in value and generates higher income.

In a world where savings accounts struggle to keep pace with rising prices and traditional investments fluctuate with market sentiment, commercial conversion offers something rare: stability. It provides a hedge against uncertainty, a buffer against economic shocks, and a pathway to long-term financial security. By converting underused commercial spaces into desirable homes, investors position themselves on the right side of economic change turning inflation from a threat into an advantage.

Recession Resilience

One of the most powerful advantages of commercial property conversion is its resilience during economic downturns. When the wider economy contracts, consumer spending tightens, and businesses begin to reduce costs, the commercial sector often feels the impact first. Retailers' close branches, offices downsize, and service providers consolidate their operations. Entire high streets can shift from vibrant commercial hubs to rows of shuttered units almost overnight. This decline is not simply a matter of reduced footfall; it reflects a deeper structural change in how people interact with physical space during periods of financial uncertainty.

Yet even as commercial demand weakens, the need for residential accommodation remains constant. People may lose jobs, change careers, or adjust their lifestyles, but they do not stop needing a place to live. Housing is not a discretionary expense; it is a fundamental human requirement. This is why residential property, particularly in the mid-market segment, tends to remain stable even when the broader economy is under pressure. Families still need homes. Young professionals still need somewhere to rent. Students still need accommodation. Life continues, and with it, the demand for shelter.

Commercial conversions tap directly into this resilience. By transforming underused commercial buildings into residential units, investors reposition their assets into a sector that is far less sensitive to economic cycles. A vacant shop or office can sit empty for months, even years, during a recession, generating no income and often deteriorating in condition. But a well-designed residential unit in the same location can achieve consistent occupancy, even in challenging times. Tenants may adjust their budgets, but they do not abandon the need for a safe, comfortable home.

Mid-market residential units are not luxury apartments, not low-end bedsits, but well-designed, affordable homes are particularly resilient. They appeal to the broadest segment of the population: working individuals, young couples, small families, and key workers. These tenants are not driven by luxury or prestige; they are driven by practicality, location, and value. During a recession, this demographic becomes even more stable, as people move away from high-end rentals and seek more affordable alternatives without compromising on quality. A commercial conversion that delivers modern, efficient, mid-priced homes becomes a magnet for this group.

This resilience extends beyond occupancy. Rental values in the mid-market segment tend to remain steady during downturn. While luxury rents may fall and low-end rents may stagnate, mid-market rents often hold firm because they reflect the true cost of living for the majority of the population. Even when wages tighten, people prioritize housing above almost everything else. This creates a buffer for investors, ensuring that income remains predictable even when other sectors experience volatility.

Commercial conversions also benefit from the fact that they often revitalize areas that have been affected by economic decline. When a vacant shop becomes a set of modern flats, it brings new residents, new spending power, and new life to the surrounding area. This creates a positive feedback loop: the conversion improves the neighborhood, and the improved neighborhood strengthens the value of the conversion.

In a world where economic cycles are becoming more unpredictable, recession resilience is not a luxury, it is a necessity. Commercial property conversion offers investors a way to protect their portfolios, stabilize their income, and build long-term security by aligning their assets with the most fundamental and enduring human need: a place to call home.

Unemployment Resilience

Another powerful advantage of commercial property conversion is its resilience during periods of rising unemployment. Economic cycles are inevitable. Industries expand and contract, companies restructure, and entire sectors can be disrupted by technology, global events, or shifts in consumer behavior. When unemployment rises, the effects ripple through the economy, influencing spending habits, confidence levels, and the stability of commercial tenants. Shops close their doors, offices reduce their workforce, and many businesses either downsize or disappear altogether. Commercial landlords often feel the impact immediately, as void periods lengthen and rental income becomes uncertain.

Commercial conversions tap directly into this stability. When you transform a commercial building into residential units, you reposition the asset into a sector that continues to function even when the economy slows down. During periods of rising unemployment, many individuals and families reassess their housing choices. Some may move out of high-end rentals to reduce costs. Others may leave expensive city-center apartments in search of more affordable options. Young professionals who once prioritized luxury amenities may shift their focus to practicality and value. In all these scenarios, well-designed mid-market homes become their natural destination.

This is where commercial conversions shine. They offer modern, efficient, sensibly priced homes that appeal to a broad demographic. These units are not competing with luxury penthouses or budget bedsits; they sit comfortably in the middle, where demand is strongest and most consistent. Even when unemployment rises, this segment remains active because it reflects the real needs of everyday people. Tenants may change jobs, retrain, or transition between roles, but they continue to prioritize housing. As long as the property is well-located, well-designed, and reasonably priced, occupancy remains strong.

There is also a psychological dimension to this resilience. During uncertain times, people seek stability. A secure home becomes even more important when other aspects of life feel unpredictable. Residential units created through commercial conversion often provide this sense of stability because they are modern, energy-efficient, and designed with contemporary living in mind. They offer comfort without excess, quality without extravagance, and affordability without compromise. This combination makes them highly attractive to tenants navigating economic uncertainty.

For investors, this resilience translates into consistent rental income, reduced void periods, and a more predictable financial outlook. While commercial landlords may struggle to find new tenants during periods of rising unemployment, residential landlords especially those offering mid-market homes often experience steady demand. This stability provides a buffer against economic shocks and helps protect long-term returns.

In a world where job markets can shift rapidly and economic conditions can change without warning, investing in assets that remain relevant regardless of employment trends is a strategic advantage. Commercial property conversion offers exactly that: a way to create homes that people will continue to need, value, and occupy, even when the wider economy is under pressure. It is a strategy built not just on opportunity, but on resilience, the kind of resilience that supports both tenants and investors through every stage of the economic cycle.

Part 1: The Opportunity

Commercial-to-residential conversion is no longer a niche strategy reserved for seasoned developers. It has become one of the most important structural shifts in the UK property market, a shift driven by planning reform, economic necessity, and the changing way people live, work, and shop. To understand why this strategy is the future, you must first understand the forces shaping it: the evolution of planning rules, the national housing shortage, the economics of development, and the type of investor best suited to this opportunity.

a. The Shift from Class E to C3

For decades, converting commercial buildings into homes required full planning permission a slow, uncertain, and often expensive process. That changed with the introduction of Class MA, which allows many Class E buildings (shops, offices, cafés, surgeries, light industrial units, and more) to be converted into C3 residential use through a streamlined Prior Approval process.

This shift is monumental. It means that thousands of buildings across the UK buildings that once required complex planning applications can now be transformed into homes with far fewer barriers. Councils still assess transport, noise, flooding, natural light, and contamination, but the principle of conversion is already accepted. The question is no longer “Should this building become housing?” but “Can it meet the technical requirements?”

This single change has unlocked an entire category of opportunity. Investors who understand Class MA can move faster, reduce planning risk, and create value in places where traditional developers see obstacles. It is one of the most investor-friendly planning reforms in modern history and it is reshaping the market.

b. The Housing Crisis and Government Policy

The UK faces a chronic housing shortage. Demand for homes far exceeds supply, and traditional housebuilding cannot keep up. At the same time, high streets have changed. Online shopping, remote work, and shifting consumer habits have left thousands of commercial units empty or underused.

Government policy is clear: repurpose what already exists. Commercial conversion aligns perfectly with this national priority. It creates homes where infrastructure already exists near transport, shops, schools, and services. It reduces pressure on greenfield land. It revitalizes declining high streets. And it delivers housing faster than ground-up development.

This is why planning reforms have consistently moved in favor of conversion. The government wants investors and developers to step into this space. They want empty buildings turned into homes. They want regeneration driven by private initiative.

For investors, this alignment with policy creates a rare advantage: a strategy that is both profitable and supported by national need.

c. Why Conversions Can Outperform Ground-Up Development

Ground-up development is expensive, slow, and heavily regulated. Land acquisition, planning risk, infrastructure requirements, and construction complexity all add time and cost. Commercial conversion, by contrast, starts with an existing structure. The foundations, walls, roof, and utilities are often already in place. This dramatically reduces build time and capital expenditure.

Conversions also benefit from:

- *Lower purchase prices: commercial buildings often sell at a discount due to limited demand.*
- *Faster planning routes: Prior Approval is quicker and more predictable than full planning.*
- *Higher value uplift: transforming a low-value commercial unit into residential space can create significant margin.*
- *Reduced construction risk: fewer unknowns compared to building from scratch.*

In many cases, the uplift created through conversion is so strong that investors can refinance, recycle capital, and move on to the next project a cycle that is far harder to achieve with ground-up development. Commercial conversion is not "easy," but it is efficient. It is strategic. And when executed well, it can outperform almost every other property strategy in terms of speed, value creation, and scalability.

d. Who This Strategy Is for And Who It Is Not For

Commercial Conversion is powerful, but it is not for everyone. It suits investors who are analytical, disciplined, and willing to learn. It rewards those who can manage professionals, make decisions based on data, and stay calm when challenges arise. It is ideal for people who want to build long-term wealth, create high-quality homes, and operate with a developer's mindset.

This strategy is not for investors who want passive income without involvement. It is not for those who avoid due diligence, dislike problem-solving, or expect quick wins without effort. Commercial buildings come with quirks, surprises, and technical requirements. Success demands structure, patience, and a willingness to engage with the process.

But for those who embrace it, commercial conversion offers something rare: a strategy that is both profitable and purposeful one that transforms communities while building long-term financial resilience.

Chapter 1: Why Commercial Conversion Is the Future

1.1 The Shift from Class E to C3

The single biggest reason commercial conversion has become one of the most powerful strategies in UK property is the dramatic shift in planning rules, a shift that fundamentally changed what investors can do with empty shops, offices, cafés, surgeries, and countless other commercial spaces. For decades, converting a commercial building into residential use required full planning permission, a process known for being slow, uncertain, and often adversarial. Councils could reject applications based on subjective interpretations of policy, local politics, or resistance to change. Many investors avoided commercial buildings entirely because the planning risk was simply too high. That changed with the introduction of Class E in 2020 and Class MA in 2021 two reforms that quietly reshaped the entire landscape.

Class E created a broad, flexible commercial use class that grouped together shops, offices, restaurants, clinics, nurseries, gyms, and more. This was the government's first major signal: they wanted commercial spaces to be more adaptable. They recognized that high streets were changing, that retail demand was declining, and that businesses needed flexibility to survive. By merging so many uses into one class, they made it easier for commercial buildings to evolve without constant planning battles.

But the real revolution came with Class MA, which allowed many Class E buildings to be converted into C3 residential use through a streamlined Prior Approval process. This is not full planning permission. It is a lighter, faster, more predictable route where the council can only assess specific technical issues such as transport, noise, flooding, contamination, and natural light. Crucially, they cannot object to the principle of converting the building into homes. That decision has already been made at national level.

This shift is profound. It means that thousands of buildings across the UK buildings that once required complex planning applications can now be transformed into homes with far fewer barriers. Investors who understand Class MA can move faster, reduce planning risk, and create value in places where traditional developers see obstacles.

Why did the government do this? Because the UK faces a severe housing shortage, and traditional housebuilding cannot keep up. At the same time, commercial vacancy rates have risen due to online shopping, remote work, and shifting consumer habits. The government needed a solution that addressed both problems at once. Commercial conversion was the answer.

By encouraging the transformation of underused commercial buildings into residential units, the government is revitalizing high streets, reducing pressure on greenfield land, and accelerating the delivery of much-needed homes. Class MA is not an accident it is a deliberate policy tool designed to unlock private-sector creativity and investment.

For investors, this creates a rare alignment: a strategy that is both profitable and supported by national policy. The rules are designed to help you succeed provided you understand them and apply them correctly.

The shift from Class E to C3 is more than a planning reform. It is the foundation of a new era in property investment, one where vision, speed, and strategic thinking are rewarded like never before.

1.2 The Housing Crisis and Government Policy

The UK's housing crisis is not a headline it is a structural reality that has been building for decades. Demand for homes has consistently outpaced supply, leaving millions priced out of ownership and councils struggling to meet even the most basic housing needs. Traditional housebuilding, while essential, simply cannot keep up with the scale or speed required. This imbalance has created one of the most powerful tailwinds behind commercial-to-residential conversion: a national need so great that government policy has shifted to actively encourage it.

At the heart of the crisis is a simple equation: the UK needs more homes than it can build through conventional means. Population growth, household formation, and urbanization have all increased demand, while planning constraints, land scarcity, and construction bottlenecks have restricted supply. Councils face enormous pressure to deliver housing targets, yet they lack the land, funding, and capacity to build at the pace required. Even when large developments are approved, they can take years sometimes a decade or more to move from planning to completion.

Meanwhile, thousands of commercial buildings sit empty. High streets have changed dramatically due to online shopping, shifting consumer habits, and the decline of traditional retail. Office demand has been reshaped by remote work and flexible working patterns. Many buildings that once served thriving businesses now stand underused or vacant, contributing to urban decline and economic stagnation.

This is where commercial conversion fits into national strategy.

The government recognized that the fastest way to deliver new homes was not to build more on greenfield land, but to repurpose what already exists. Commercial buildings are already connected to utilities, transport, and local infrastructure. They are located in town centres, near shops, schools, and services. They occupy land that is already developed, meaning no loss of green space and no lengthy battles over land allocation.

By encouraging the transformation of commercial units into residential homes,

The government achieves multiple objectives at once:

- *Revitalizing high streets by bringing residents back into town centres.*
- *Reducing pressure on councils to approve large, controversial developments.*
- *Delivering homes faster through Prior Approval rather than full planning.*
- *Supporting sustainability goals by reusing existing structures.*
- *Stimulating private investment in areas that need regeneration.*

This alignment between policy and opportunity is why Class MA exists. It is not a loophole it is a deliberate tool designed to unlock private-sector creativity and accelerate housing delivery. Councils may still assess technical matters such as noise, transport, flooding, and natural light, but they cannot object to the principle of conversion. The message is clear: the government wants commercial buildings to become homes.

For investors, this creates a unique environment. Unlike many property strategies that operate against the grain of policy, commercial conversion moves with it. You are not fighting the system you are participating in a national solution. And because the need is so great, the opportunity is not short-term. It is structural, long-term, and deeply embedded in the future of UK housing.

Commercial conversion is not just profitable. It is purposeful. It is aligned with government priorities, community needs, and economic reality. And that alignment is one of the strongest reasons this strategy is the future.

1.3 Why Conversions Can Outperform Ground-Up Development

One of the most compelling reasons commercial conversions is rising in popularity is its ability to outperform traditional ground-up development across almost every major metric: speed, cost, planning risk, sustainability, and profit potential. While new-build projects will always have their place, the economics and efficiency of conversion give investors a strategic edge that is difficult to match.

The first major advantage is speed. Ground-up development is slow by nature. It requires land acquisition, full planning permission, demolition, foundation work, structural construction, and extensive compliance checks. Even a small new-build scheme can take 18–36 months from purchase to completion. In contrast, commercial conversions often begin with a solid shell: foundations, walls, roof, utilities, and access are already in place. This dramatically reduces construction time. Many conversions can be completed within 6–12 months, allowing investors to recycle capital faster and move on to the next project. In a market where momentum is everything, speed becomes a competitive advantage.

The second advantage is cost efficiency. Buildings from scratch is expensive. Material costs, labor, groundworks, and infrastructure contributions all add up. Commercial conversions, however, reuse existing structures, reducing the need for heavy construction. While internal reconfiguration, fire safety upgrades, and insulation improvements are still required, the overall cost per square foot is often significantly lower than new-build. This cost efficiency directly increases profit margins and reduces financial exposure.

Planning risk is another area where conversions shine. Ground-up development requires full planning permission, which can be unpredictable and time-consuming. Councils may reject applications based on design, density, traffic impact, or local politics. Appeals can drag on for months. Commercial conversion under Class MA, however, uses the Prior Approval route. This is not full planning. The council can only assess specific technical matters such as transport, noise, flooding, contamination, and natural light. They cannot object to the principle of converting the building into homes. This dramatically reduces planning uncertainty and gives investors a clearer path to approval.

Sustainability is also a major factor. Reusing existing buildings is inherently more environmentally friendly than demolishing and rebuilding. It reduces waste, preserves embodied carbon, and aligns with national sustainability goals. Many councils now favor conversion over demolition because it supports greener development practices. Investors who embrace conversion are not only benefiting financially, but they are also contributing to a more sustainable built environment.

Finally, conversions often offer superior profit potential. Because commercial buildings are frequently undervalued due to limited demand, investors can acquire them at favorable prices. When combined with lower build costs and faster timelines, the uplift created through conversion can be substantial. In many cases, the end value of the completed residential units far exceeds the total project cost, enabling refinancing and capital recycling a cycle that is far harder to achieve with new-build development.

In short, commercial conversions outperform ground-up development because they are faster, cheaper, lower risk, more sustainable, and often more profitable. They allow investors to create high-quality homes while leveraging existing structures, planning reforms, and market inefficiencies. For those who understand the process, conversion is not just an alternative to new-build it is a strategic upgrade.

1.4 Who This Strategy Is for and Who It Is Not For

Commercial-to-residential conversion is one of the most powerful strategies in modern UK property, but it is not a universal fit. Like any sophisticated investment approach, it rewards certain types of people and exposes the weaknesses of others. Understanding whether this strategy aligns with your personality, skills, and long-term goals is just as important as understanding planning rules or finance structures. This section will help you recognize where you stand and whether commercial conversion is the right path for you.

Commercial conversion is ideal for investors who are strategic thinkers. These are people who enjoy solving problems, analyzing buildings, and making decisions based on evidence rather than emotion. They understand that every commercial property is unique, with its own quirks, constraints, and opportunities. They are comfortable working with professionals, asking questions, and learning continuously. If you enjoy the process of understanding how things work from planning policy to structural layouts, this strategy will feel natural.

It is also well-suited to investors who value control and creativity. Unlike traditional buy-to-let, where you inherit a finished product, commercial conversion allows you to shape the outcome. You decide the layout, the design, the specification, and the final use. You influence the value you create. Investors who enjoy adding value through design, optimization, and vision thrive in this environment. They see potential where others see problems, and they are motivated by the transformation process.

Another group who excels in commercial conversion are those who are comfortable managing teams. This strategy involves coordinating solicitors, surveyors, planning consultants, contractors, and lenders. You don't need to be an expert in every field, but you must be able to communicate clearly, make decisions, and keep the project moving. Investors who can lead, delegate, and maintain structure will find this strategy both rewarding and scalable.

Commercial conversion is also a strong fit for investors who want to build long-term wealth rather than chase quick wins. The ability to refinance, recycle capital, and hold high-quality residential units in strong locations makes this strategy ideal for those who think in decades, not months. If your goal is to build a resilient, income-producing portfolio that grows in value over time, commercial conversion aligns perfectly with that vision. However, this strategy is not for everyone.

It is not for investors who want passive income without involvement. Commercial conversion requires decisions, oversight, and engagement. It is not a "hands-off" strategy, especially during the acquisition and construction phases. It is not for those who avoid due diligence or dislike detail. Commercial buildings come with technical requirements fire safety, natural light, structural integrity, planning constraints. Investors who rush, cut corners, or rely on guesswork will struggle.

It is not for people who panic easily. Every project has surprises. Walls hide issues, surveys reveal defects, contractors raise variations. Investors who remain calm, solution-focused, and disciplined are the ones who succeed. And finally, it is not for those who expect guaranteed outcomes. Property carries risk. Markets shift. Costs fluctuate. Planning rules evolve. Successful investors embrace uncertainty and manage it intelligently. Commercial conversion is a strategy for thinkers, planners, problem-solvers, and creators. If that sounds like you, you are in the right place and the opportunities ahead are extraordinary.

Chapter 2: Understanding Commercial Buildings

2.1 Types of Commercial Buildings: Shops, Offices, Warehouses, Pubs, Banks, Mixed-Use

Commercial buildings come in many shapes, sizes, and histories and each one presents a different opportunity when converting to residential use. To succeed in commercial conversion, you must understand how these buildings were originally designed, how they functioned in their commercial life, and how their physical characteristics influence their suitability for housing. Not all commercial buildings are equal. Some convert beautifully with minimal intervention; others require creativity, engineering, or a complete imagination of the space. This section breaks down the most common building types you will encounter and what they mean for your strategy.

Shops (Retail Units)

Shops are among the most accessible and common commercial buildings for conversion. Traditionally designed with large front windows, open floor areas, and storage rooms at the back, they often offer excellent natural light and straightforward layouts. Many small shops come with unused lofts or deep rear sections that can be reconfigured into flats. Their biggest advantage is location: shops sit on high streets, corner plots, and mixed-use areas where residential demand is strong. The main challenges include noise from nearby businesses, limited rear access, and the need to create compliant escape routes. Still, for many first-time converters, shops represent the perfect entry point.

Offices

Office buildings vary widely, from small two-storey units to large multi-floor blocks. They are typically designed with open-plan layouts, suspended ceilings, and generous floor plates features that make them highly adaptable for residential use. Offices often have strong structural integrity, good ceiling heights, and existing service routes for electrics and plumbing. Their main challenge is natural light: deep floor plates can create dark internal zones that are unsuitable for bedrooms. Acoustic performance is another consideration, as office floors were not built with residential noise separation in mind. When these issues are addressed, offices can deliver high-density, high-value conversions.

Warehouses

Warehouses offer large, flexible spaces with high ceilings and robust structures. Originally designed for storage and logistics, they often feature steel frames, wide spans, and minimal internal walls. This makes them ideal for creative conversions such as loft-style apartments or co-living spaces. However, warehouses can present challenges: limited windows, industrial-grade flooring, and the need for significant insulation upgrades. They may also be located in areas with noise or traffic considerations. When handled correctly, warehouse conversions can produce some of the most striking and desirable residential units.

Pubs

Pubs are full of character timber beams, brick fireplaces, quirky layouts but they also come with emotional and community significance. Many pubs include large ground-floor bar areas and upper-floor accommodation, making them suitable for HMOs or co-living schemes. Their charm is a selling point, but their age can hide issues such as damp, outdated electrics, or structural wear. Pubs often require careful design to balance heritage with modern living standards. When done well, they create unique homes with strong market appeal.

Banks

Banks were built to be secure, solid, and imposing. Thick walls, high ceilings, and grand frontages make them architecturally impressive. Internally, however, they may include vaults, reinforced rooms, and awkward layouts. Converting a bank requires creativity and sometimes structural intervention, but the end result can be premium apartments with distinctive character. Their central locations make them highly desirable once transformed.

Mixed-Use Buildings

Mixed-use buildings combine commercial space on the ground floor with residential or office space above. These are often the easiest to convert because part of the building is already residential. The main task is reconfiguring the commercial element and ensuring compliance across the entire structure. Mixed-use conversions offer strong returns and reduced planning friction.

Understanding these building types of their strengths, limitations, and hidden potential is the foundation of successful commercial conversion. Each one tells a story. Your job is to rewrite it into a home.

2.2 Typical Layouts and Constraints

To convert a commercial building successfully, you must understand how these structures are put together. Unlike residential homes, which follow fairly predictable patterns, commercial buildings vary widely depending on their original purpose. Their internal layouts, structural systems, and service arrangements all influence what is possible and what is not when designing new residential units. This section breaks down the key physical characteristics you will encounter and how they shape your conversion strategy.

Floor Plates

The “floor plate” refers to the shape and size of each level. Shops and small offices often have shallow floor plates, meaning the distance from the front to the back of the building is relatively short. This is ideal for residential conversion because natural light can reach most areas. Larger offices and warehouses, however, may have deep floor plates with large central zones far from windows. These dark internal areas cannot be used for habitable rooms under residential standards. They may become corridors, storage, plant rooms, or internal bathrooms, but they limit how many units you can create.

Understanding the floor plate early helps you avoid overestimating the building's potential.

Ceiling Heights

Commercial buildings typically have higher ceilings than residential homes. Offices often feature suspended ceilings hiding ductwork and wiring, while shops and warehouses may have generous head heights designed for display or storage. Higher ceilings are a major advantage in conversion: they create a sense of space, allow for mezzanines in some cases, and make layouts more flexible. However, ceiling height can also reveal constraints. Removing a suspended ceiling may expose beams, pipes, or uneven surfaces that require additional work. In older buildings, ceiling heights may vary between rooms, affecting design consistency.

Access Points

Access is one of the most overlooked aspects of commercial conversion. Many commercial buildings were designed with a single main entrance for customers and a rear service door for staff. Residential use, however, requires secure, private access for each unit. You may need to create new entrances, reconfigure staircases, or separate commercial and residential access in mixed-use buildings. Fire regulations also require protected escape routes, which can influence where walls, doors, and corridors must be placed. A building with poor access can still be converted, but it may require creative design and structural intervention.

Service Cores

In commercial buildings, utilities such as toilets, kitchens, risers, and mechanical systems are often grouped into a "service core." This centralized cluster makes sense for offices and shops but can be restrictive for residential layouts. You may need to extend plumbing, relocate bathrooms, or add new risers to serve multiple flats. Understanding where the service core sits and how easily it can be adapted is essential for accurate cost planning. In some buildings, the service core becomes the backbone of your design; in others, it becomes a constraint you must work around.

Fire Escapes

Commercial buildings often include external fire escapes, internal stairwells, or protected corridors designed for staff and customers. Residential standards are stricter. You may need to upgrade fire doors, add sprinklers, create protected lobbies, or redesign escape routes entirely. Fire safety is one of the most significant technical considerations in conversion, and the existing escape strategy will heavily influence your layout options.

Understanding these internal characteristics is the key to unlocking a building's potential. The more you learn to read a commercial layout, the faster you will identify opportunities and avoid costly mistakes.

2.3 Which Types Are Most Suitable for Conversion

Not every commercial building is created equal, and the investors who succeed in this space are the ones who learn to recognize suitability at a glance. The goal is not simply to find a building that can be converted, but one that can be converted efficiently, profitably, and with minimal friction. Suitability is shaped by four core factors: natural light, structural logic, planning flexibility, and market demand. When these elements align, a building becomes a high-potential asset rather than a costly puzzle.

Buildings With Predictable Structural Logic

Some commercial buildings were designed with simplicity in mind straight walls, regular column spacing, and clear load paths. These buildings convert beautifully because their structure doesn't fight your design. Small offices, corner shops, and many mixed-use buildings fall into this category. Their layout allows you to position kitchens, bathrooms, and bedrooms without battling awkward beams or irregular spans. Predictability reduces engineering costs and speeds up design work, making these buildings ideal for investors who want clean, efficient projects.

Buildings With Strong Natural Light Distribution

Natural light is one of the biggest determinants of suitability. Buildings with windows on multiple sides, shallow depths, or large glazed frontages are far easier to convert into compliant residential units. This is why former banks, small offices, and high-street shops often outperform warehouses or deep-plan retail units. When light reaches most of the floor area, you can create more habitable rooms without resorting to expensive structural changes. Light is not just a design feature, it is a compliance requirement, and buildings that naturally meet this standard are inherently more profitable.

Buildings Already Embedded in Residential Demand Zones

Some commercial buildings sit in locations where people already want to live high streets, transport corridors, neighborhood centres, and mixed-use districts. These buildings benefit from build-in demand. Tenants want to live near shops, buses, cafés, and services. Buyers want walkable neighborhoods. When a building is already positioned in a desirable area, your conversion becomes easier to rent, easier to sell, and easier to refinance. This is why small shops, banks, and mixed-use buildings often outperform industrial units on the outskirts of town.

Buildings With Planning Flexibility Under Class MA

Suitability is not just physical, it is regulatory. Some buildings glide through Prior Approval because they sit outside Article 4 zones, have no flood-risk complications, and meet noise and access requirements. Offices and shops in stable commercial zones often fall into this category. Their planning history is clean, their use class is clear, and their location aligns with government objectives. These buildings offer smoother approvals and fewer surprises, making them ideal for investors who want predictable outcomes.

Buildings With Minimal "Legacy Problems"

Some commercial buildings carry baggage: asbestos, structural movement, heritage restrictions, or decades of ad-hoc alterations. Others are clean, modern, and straightforward. The most suitable buildings are those with minimal legacy issues modern offices, post-war shops, and well-maintained mixed-use blocks. They require less investigative work, fewer specialist reports, and fewer contingency allowances. This directly improves profitability and reduces risk.

The Sweet Spot
The most suitable buildings for conversion are those that combine:
- *Simple structure*
- *Strong natural light*
- *Good location*
- *Planning clarity*
- *Minimal legacy issues*

These buildings don't just convert well they convert profitably, predictably, and with far less stress.

2.4 Red Flags to Avoid at Building Type Level

Not every commercial building is a hidden gem. Some are ticking financial time bombs disguised as opportunities. The most successful commercial-conversion investors are not the ones who find the most buildings, they are the ones who learn to walk away from the wrong ones quickly. At building-type level, certain red flags should immediately raise your guard. These issues don't just increase cost; they can destroy feasibility, kill planning prospects, or trap you in a project that bleeds money. This section highlights the deal-killers you must recognize before committing.

a. Structural Red Flags Hidden in Older Buildings
Some commercial buildings, especially pubs, Victorian shops, and pre-war banks carry structural risks that are invisible to the untrained eye. Bowed brickwork, sagging floors, and historic movement can signal deep-rooted issues that require steel reinforcement or partial rebuilds. Timber-framed upper floors in old pubs often hide rot, beetle infestation, or decades of DIY alterations. These aren't cosmetic problems; they are structural liabilities. If a building type is known for age-related deterioration, assume nothing and investigate everything.

b. Contamination Risks in Industrial and Warehouse Buildings
Warehouses, workshops, and light-industrial units often come with contamination risks that can turn a simple conversion into an

environmental headache. Oil-soaked floors, asbestos roofing, chemical residues, or underground tanks can trigger mandatory remediation. These costs escalate fast and can wipe out your margin before you even start. If a building's previous use involved machinery, chemicals, or heavy storage, contamination must be treated as a serious red flag until proven otherwise.

c. Planning Restrictions Linked to Community Value
Some building types of especially pubs, banks, and post offices carry community value designations. Even if they fall under Class E, councils may resist their loss because they serve (or historically served) a social function. A pub with an ACV (Asset of Community Value) listing can become a planning battle you don't want. Banks in conservation areas may face heritage restrictions that limit external changes. If a building type has emotional or historical significance locally, expect resistance and delays.

d. Layouts That Fight Residential Logic
Certain commercial layouts simply don't translate well into homes. Deep-plan retail units with no rear windows, banks with reinforced vaults in the centre, and warehouses with minimal openings can force you into awkward, inefficient designs. If the building's shape makes it difficult to create compliant bedrooms, protected escape routes, or logical circulation, the project becomes a constant compromise. A building that fights your layout is a building that drains your budget.

e. Hidden Costs in "Character" Buildings
Character sells but character also costs. Pubs with ornate façades, banks with stone columns, and heritage buildings with decorative brickwork may require specialist contractors, conservation officers, or bespoke materials. These costs multiply quickly. A building with charm can become a financial trap if every repair requires heritage-approved methods. If the building type screams "historic," assume higher costs until proven otherwise.

f. Buildings in Declining Commercial Zones
Some commercial buildings are cheap for a reason. If the surrounding

area is declining, has high vacancies, or lacks residential demand, even the best conversion will struggle. A building type located in a dying retail strip or industrial estate may not attract the tenants or buyers you need. Suitability is not just about the building it's about the context it sits in.

The smartest investors learn to spot these red flags early. Knowing when to walk away is just as valuable as knowing when to proceed.

Chapter 3: Sourcing & Initial Appraisal

3.1 Finding Tired or Underused Assets

The most profitable commercial conversions begin long before planning, design, or construction. They begin with the ability to spot buildings that others overlook the tired, underused, or forgotten assets hiding in plain sight. These buildings are not always advertised as "development opportunities." In fact, the best ones are rare. They sit quietly on high streets, in neighborhood centres, or at the edge of commercial zones, waiting for someone with vision to recognize their potential. This section teaches you how to identify them.

Look for Buildings Showing Physical Fatigue

A tired building often reveals itself through subtle signs: peeling signage, faded paint, boarded-up windows, or a shopfront that hasn't been updated in decades. These are not cosmetic issues, they are clues. A neglected exterior usually signals a landlord who has stopped investing, a tenant who is struggling, or a building that has outlived its commercial purpose. When you see a property that looks like it has been left behind by the surrounding area, you've found a potential conversion candidate.

Track Vacancy Patterns, Not Just Individual Vacancies

One empty shop tells you very little. Three empty shops on the same parade tell you everything. Clusters of vacancy indicate structural change shifting footfall, declining retail demand, or a high street transitioning toward residential use. These areas often become fertile ground for Class MA conversions because councils recognize the need to repurpose space. When you see multiple "To Let" boards that never seem to come down, you're looking at a location where commercial demand has weakened enough to create opportunity.
Identify Ownership Clues That Signal Motivation

Some buildings practically advertise that the owner is ready to sell if you know what to look for.

Key signs include:

- *Long-term vacant units with no attempt at refurbishment*
- *Outdated letting boards from agencies that no longer operate*
- *Properties held by pension funds or elderly landlords who may prefer a clean exit*
- *Units with repeated short-term tenants, indicating instability*

Land Registry data can reveal whether the owner is an individual, a company, or an estate each with different motivations. A building owned by a dissolved company or a deceased estate often becomes a prime acquisition target.

Spot Buildings That No Longer Fit Their Surroundings

Some commercial buildings simply don't make sense anymore. A large bank branch on a high street where banking has been moved online. A warehouse surrounded by new housing estates. A pub in an area where footfall has shifted. When a building's original purpose no longer aligns with the neighborhood's current reality, conversion becomes the logical next step. These "misfit buildings" are often the easiest to justify under Class MA because their commercial relevance has faded.

Pay Attention to Signs of Distress Behind the Scenes

Distress isn't always visible from the outside. Look for:

- *Business rates arrears*
- *Auction listings with vague descriptions*
- *Tenants operating reduced hours*
- *Shops with minimal stock or temporary displays*

These subtle indicators often point to landlords who are open to negotiation sometimes at significant discounts.

The Real Skill: Seeing What Others Miss

Finding tired or underused assets is not about luck. It's about training your eyes to read the street, interpret the clues, and understand the story behind each building. The more you walk, observe, and analyze, the more opportunities you will uncover long before they hit the open market.

3.2 Reading Commercial Listings and Understanding Yields

Most beginners scroll through commercial listings without truly understanding what they're looking at. They see square footage, rental income, and an asking price but they don't see the story behind the numbers. Commercial listings are written in a coded language, and once you learn to interpret that language, you can instantly separate genuine opportunities from overpriced distractions. This section teaches you how to read listings like a professional investor.

Start With the Yield But Don't Be Fooled by It

Commercial agents love to advertise yields: "8% yield," "10% yield," "12% investment opportunity."

But here's the truth: the higher the advertised yield, the weaker the commercial demand usually is.

A high yield often signals:

• *A struggling tenant*

• *A declining high street*

• *A short lease*

• *A landlord trying to offload risk*

For conversion investors, this is not necessarily bad, but it must be understood. A high yield doesn't mean the building is cheap; it means the commercial value is low. Your job is to determine whether the residential value is high enough to justify the purchase.

Decode Agent Terminology

Commercial agents use language that reveals far more than they intend.

Key phrases include:

• *"Tenant relocating"; often means the tenant is leaving because the location no longer works.*

• *"Suitable for a variety of uses"; usually means the building is empty and the agent is fishing.*

• *"Reversionary potential"; the rent is below market value but only matters if you plan to keep it commercial.*

• *"Sold with vacant possession"; ideal for conversion; no tenant to remove.*

• *"Long lease remaining"; bad for conversion; you may be stuck with a tenant for years.*

Once you understand these phrases, listings become far easier to interpret.

Analyze the Lease, Not Just the Rent

Commercial value is driven by the lease. A building with a strong tenant on a long lease will command a higher price even if the building itself is tired. For conversion investors, this can be a trap. You don't want a 15-year lease with upward-only rent reviews. You want flexibility.

Key red flags include:

• *Long leases (anything over 5 years remaining)*

• *Protected tenancies under the Landlord and Tenant Act 1954*

• *Break clauses that favor the tenant*

If the lease locks you out of the building, the deal is dead. Check Whether the Asking Price Reflects Reality

Commercial asking prices are often inflated because sellers anchor their expectations to outdated valuations.

To determine true value, compare:

• *Price per square foot against similar buildings*

• *Vacancy duration (longer vacancy = lower real value)*

• *Condition (tired buildings should be discounted)*

• *Location demand (footfall, transport, residential desirability)*

If the asking price is based on commercial value but the commercial demand is collapsing, you have negotiating power.

Look for Clues Hidden in the Numbers

A listing that shows:

• *Low rent*

• *High yield*

• *Long vacancy*

• *No recent refurbishments*
...is telling you the building is underperforming commercially which is exactly where conversion opportunities live.

The Real Skill: Reading Between the Lines
Commercial listings are not just advertisements; they are diagnostic reports. Once you learn to interpret yields, decode agent language, and analyze leases, you will see opportunities others miss and avoid the traps that catch inexperienced investors.

3.3 Speaking the Language of Commercial Agents

Commercial agents operate in a world that feels very different from residential property. Their conversations revolve around leases, covenants, yields, and risk profiles not bedrooms, décor, or "potential." If you want them to take you seriously, you must learn to communicate in a way that signals you understand their environment. The moment an agent senses that you speak their language, the dynamic shifts. You stop being a curious browser and become someone worth calling when a landlord whispers, "I want this gone quietly."

The first thing to understand is that commercial agents filter people fast. They speak to dozens of investors every week, and most of them are vague, unfocused, or simply curious. Agents don't have time to educate buyers. They want clarity. They want confidence. They want to know you can perform. When you open a conversation with precision asking about the passing rent, the unexpired lease term, or whether the tenant is inside or outside the 1954 Act you immediately separate yourself from the crowd. You're not trying to impress them; you're showing them you understand the fundamentals.

Commercial agents also respond to buyers who know exactly what they want. When you say, "I specialize in converting Class E buildings to residential," you give them a clear box to put you in. That box is important. It tells them which deals to send you and which ones to ignore. It also reassures them that you're not a time-waster who will disappear halfway through a negotiation. Focus builds trust, and trust is the currency that unlocks off-market opportunities.

Your tone matters just as much as your terminology. Agents want to hear that you can move decisively. They want to know you have solicitors ready, finance lined up, and the ability to make a decision without dragging things out. You don't need to brag; you simply need to communicate like someone who has done this before. A calm, confident tone carries more weight than any sales pitch.

There are also certain questions that instantly elevate you in an agent's eyes. When you ask how long the unit has been vacant, whether the landlord has attempted to re-let it, or what the seller's motivation is, you're demonstrating that you understand the commercial story behind the building. You're not just looking at square footage you're analyzing the situation. Agents remember investors who ask intelligent questions because those are investors who close deals.

A small number of bullet points help reinforce this perception without overwhelming the narrative:

- *Agents prioritize buyers who communicate clearly and make decisions quickly.*
- *They trust investors who understand leases, yields, and tenant positions.*
- *They value professionalism far more than enthusiasm.*

Professionalism is the final piece. Returning calls promptly, honoring your word, and not renegotiating without cause builds a reputation that agents talk about. When they know you're reliable, you become the person they call first often before a property is photographed, listed, or even publicly discussed.

Speaking the language of commercial agents is not about pretending to be an expert. It's about showing that you respect their world, understand their priorities, and can operate at their level. Once you do that, the doors to off-market deals open naturally.

3.4 Quick "Back-of-an-Envelope" Feasibility Checks

Before you spend a penny on architects, surveys, or planning consultants, you need a fast way to judge whether a building is even worth pursuing. Experienced investors don't dive into full analysis

immediately. They run quick, instinctive checks the kind of rapid calculations you can do while standing outside the building, walking through it for the first time, or reading a listing on your phone. These "back-of-an-envelope" assessments don't replace detailed due diligence, but they stop you wasting time on deals that will never work.
The first mental model is simple: Does the building make residential sense?
You're looking for a basic alignment between the building's shape, its light, its access, and the number of units you could realistically create. If the floor plate is too deep, the windows too few, or the access too awkward, no amount of design magic will fix it. You don't need drawings to see this you just need to imagine where the bedrooms would go, where the kitchens could sit, and whether the escape routes make sense. If you can't picture a compliant layout in your mind, the deal is already weak.
The second check is financial. You want a quick feel for whether the numbers could stack before you start modelling anything. Most investors use a simple rule of thumb: Can the total cost (purchase + works + fees) come in at roughly 65–70% of the end value?
This isn't a rigid formula, but it gives you a sense of whether the uplift is strong enough to justify the effort. If the asking price alone is already 70% of the likely GDV, you're fighting an uphill battle. If the building is cheap relative to its potential residential value, you may have something worth exploring.

A few quick figures help sharpen this instinct:

- *A rough build cost per square foot based on the building type*
- *A conservative estimate of the number of units you could create*
- *A realistic local sales or rental value*

You're not trying to be precise you're trying to see whether the deal survives a cold, honest first pass.
The third check is planning-related. You want to know whether the building sits in a location where Prior Approval is likely to be smooth. If it's in an Article 4 area, a flood zone, or a conservation area with strict design controls, you need to pause. None of these are automatic deal-killers, but they change the risk profile. A quick look at the

council's planning map or a glance at nearby conversions can tell you whether the area is friendly to residential change.

The final check is demand. Even the best conversion fails if the finished units don't appeal to the market. You want to know whether people actually want to live in that location. A quick scan of rental listings, local amenities, and footfall patterns gives you a sense of whether the area has life. If the high street is dying, the transport links are weak, or the neighborhood feels disconnected, the exit becomes harder.

These rapid checks don't give you certainty they give you direction. They tell you whether to walk away, dig deeper, or move fast. Mastering them saves you time, protects your capital, and sharpens your instincts long before the professionals get involved.

3.5 When to Walk Away Early

One of the most valuable skills in commercial conversion is knowing when to walk away. Not after you've paid for surveys. Not after you've spent weeks modelling layouts. Early. The best investors don't fall in love with buildings; they fall in love with numbers, logic, and feasibility. They know that every hour spent on a dead deal is an hour stolen from the deal that could have changed everything. Walking away early is not a sign of weakness, it's a sign of discipline.

The first warning sign is when the building fights you from the moment you step inside. Some buildings have a natural flow: the light makes sense, the access is workable, and you can intuitively picture where the units would go. Others feel awkward the second you enter. Deep, windowless zones. Strange structural spans. Staircases in the wrong place. Escape routes that would require miracles. If your brain is already trying to "force" a layout during the viewing, that's your cue. A good building invites solutions; a bad one demands compromises.

Another early red flag is when the numbers feel strained even before you've done any detailed calculations. If the asking price is inflated, the commercial rent is artificially propping up the valuation, or the GDV in that area is capped, you're starting from a weak position. A quick mental check purchase plus works plus fees versus end value should give you a sense of whether the uplift is even worth chasing. If the margin feels thin at first glance, it will only get thinner once reality kicks in.

Planning context is another area where early decisions matter. A building in an Article 4 zone, a conservation area with strict design controls, or a flood-risk location may still be viable, but the risk profile changes dramatically. If you're early in your journey, these complications can drain your time and energy. Even experienced developers sometimes walk away from buildings that sit in planning grey zones because the uncertainty outweighs the potential reward. When the planning environment feels hostile, trust that instinct.

There are also buildings that carry invisible baggage. Long leases with protected tenants. Complex ownership structures. Freeholds tied up in pension funds. Properties with historic disputes, restrictive covenants, or unresolved title issues. These problems rarely get smaller with time. If the agent hesitates when you ask about the lease, or the ownership history looks messy, that's a sign to pause. Complexity is not always a deal-killer, but it is always a cost.

A few subtle cues also help you recognize dead ends early:

- *If the agent cannot articulate the landlord's motivation, the seller may not be serious.*
- *If the building has been on the market for years with no price movement, something is wrong.*
- *If every solution you imagine requires expensive intervention, the building is telling you to walk away.*

The truth is simple: great deals feel workable early. They don't require mental gymnastics, heroic assumptions, or blind optimism. When a building shows you its problems upfront, believe it. Walking away early protects your time, your capital, and your emotional bandwidth and it keeps you ready for the deal that truly deserves your attention.

Part 2: Planning, Law & Compliance

Commercial-to-residential conversion is one of the most powerful strategies in modern UK property, but it is also one of the most misunderstood. Many investors focus on sourcing, numbers, and construction, yet overlook the single factor that determines whether a project lives or dies planning. Planning is not a box-ticking exercise. It is the framework that shapes what you can build, how fast you can build it, and how much value you can ultimately create. If you misunderstand the rules, you risk buying a building you cannot convert, spending money on consultants you never needed, or entering a planning battle you cannot win.

Part 2 exists to remove that uncertainty. It gives you a clear, practical understanding of the legal and regulatory landscape that governs commercial conversion in England. This is not a legal textbook. It is a strategic guide written in plain English that shows you how to navigate planning with confidence, speed, and intelligence. By the end of this part, you will understand the rules well enough to make informed decisions, avoid unnecessary risk, and communicate with planners, consultants, and architects like someone who has been doing this for years.

Planning is often portrayed as unpredictable, but in reality, it becomes predictable once you understand its logic. The government wants more homes. Councils want safe, compliant development. Investors want clarity. When you understand how these interests interact, planning stops feeling like a barrier and starts feeling like a tool one that can accelerate your project rather than slow it down.

To give you that clarity, Part 2 is divided into five focused chapters, each addressing a critical piece of the planning puzzle. These chapters build on each other, moving from the fundamentals to the nuances, and finally to the strategic decisions that separate successful investors from frustrated ones.

a. Class MA Explained in Plain English

Class MA is the beating heart of commercial-to-residential conversion. It is the permitted development right (PDR) that allows you to convert Class E buildings shops, offices, banks, cafés, gyms, and more into residential use without applying for full planning permission. But while Class MA is powerful, it is also widely misunderstood. Many investors know the headline "you can convert commercial buildings into flats" but they don't understand the criteria, the limitations, or the practical realities.

This chapter breaks Class MA down into simple, accessible language. It explains what qualifies, what doesn't, and why. It covers the rules around vacancies, floor space, natural light, noise, transport, contamination, and flooding not as abstract regulations, but as real-world considerations that shape your design and your feasibility. You will learn how councils assess Class MA applications, what they can and cannot object to, and how to position your project for smooth approval. By the end of this chapter, Class MA will feel like a tool you can use confidently, not a legal maze you're afraid to enter.

b. Prior Approval vs Full Planning

One of the biggest strategic decisions in any conversion project is choosing the right planning route. Many investors assume that Prior Approval is always the best option because it is faster and more predictable. But that is not always true. Some buildings are better suited to full planning. Some projects require a hybrid approach. And some investors waste months pursuing the wrong route simply because they don't understand the difference.

This chapter explains Prior Approval and full planning in a way that makes the choice obvious. It shows you what Prior Approval actually covers, what councils are allowed to assess, and how the process differs from a full planning application. It also explains when full planning is the smarter route, for example, when you want to add floors, extend the building, change the façade, or reconfigure the structure. You will learn how to read a building and instantly know which route gives you the best chance of success.

c. The Removal of the 1,500 sqm Limit and What It Means

For years, Class MA was capped at 1,500 sqm. This meant that large offices, department stores, and commercial blocks were off-limits for PDR conversion. That limit has now been removed, a change that has opened the door to some of the most exciting opportunities in the market.

This chapter explains the significance of that change. It shows you how larger buildings can now be approached under Class MA, what new opportunities this creates, and what new risks come with scale. It also explores how developers are using this change to unlock multi-unit schemes, co-living projects, and large-scale residential blocks that were previously impossible under PDR. If you want to understand where the market is heading, this chapter gives you the roadmap.

d. Local Nuances and Council Attitudes

Planning is national, but councils interpret rules through their own lens. Some councils embrace Class MA because they want to revitalize their high streets. Others resist it because they fear losing commercial space. Some are efficient and pragmatic. Others are slow, political, or risk-averse.

This chapter teaches you how to read a council's attitude before you submit anything. You will learn how to analyze past decisions, interpret planning language, and understand the subtle signals that reveal whether a council is supportive or obstructive. You will also learn how to adapt your strategy to local conditions, choosing the right consultants, framing your application correctly, and anticipating objections before they arise. This chapter gives you the ability to navigate planning culture, not just planning law.

e. When PDR Is Not the Right Route

Permitted Development Rights are powerful, but they are not universal. Some buildings are better suited to full planning. Some projects require design freedom that PDR cannot provide. And some investors get trapped because they assume PDR is always the fastest or safest route.

This chapter explains when PDR becomes a limitation rather than an advantage. It covers heritage buildings, complex structures, mixed-use blocks, and scenarios where PDR creates design constraints that harm the final product. It also shows you how to recognize when full planning gives you more value, more flexibility, or a cleaner path to approval.

By the end of Part 2, readers will feel legally literate, strategically confident, and fully equipped to navigate planning with the clarity of a seasoned developer. They will understand not just the rules, but the mindset required to use those rules to their advantage.

Chapter 4: Permitted Development Rights (PDR)

4.1 Class MA Explained in Plain English

Class MA is the engine behind the modern commercial-to-residential boom. It is the permitted development right that has transformed empty shops, offices, banks, cafés, and countless other commercial spaces into much-needed homes across England. Yet despite its power, Class MA is often misunderstood. Many investors know the headline "you can convert commercial buildings into flats without full planning permission" but few understand what that actually means in practice. This chapter strips away the jargon and explains Class MA in the simplest, most practical terms.

At its core, ***Class MA allows you to change a building from Class E (commercial) to Class C3 (residential) through a process called Prior Approval***. This is not full planning permission. It is a streamlined route where the council can only assess a limited set of technical issues. They cannot debate the principle of turning the building into homes. They cannot argue about "loss of retail." They cannot reject the application because they prefer the building to stay commercial. The government has already made that decision for them.

To qualify for Class MA, a building must meet a few basic criteria. It must have been in Class E use for at least two years, and it must have been vacant for at least three months before you apply. These rules exist to ensure that genuinely underused commercial space is being repurposed, not active businesses being displaced. The building must also sit outside certain restricted zones, for example, some conservation areas, national parks, and Article 4 areas where councils have removed PDR rights. These exceptions are not common, but they matter. Once a building qualifies, the council's role becomes narrow. Under Prior Approval, they can only assess specific technical matters such as transport impact, noise, contamination, flooding, and natural light. These are practical concerns, not political ones. If your building meets technical standards, the council must approve the conversion. This is why Class MA has become the backbone of commercial-to-residential development: it removes the uncertainty that often comes with full planning.

Class MA also gives investors a powerful advantage: speed. Prior Approval decisions are typically made within 56 days, which means you can move from acquisition to construction far faster than with traditional planning routes. This speed reduces holding costs, accelerates refinancing, and allows you to recycle capital more efficiently.

There are, however, limits. Class MA does not allow you to extend the building, add floors, or make major external alterations. It is a conversion right, not a redevelopment right. If your vision requires structural changes or significant façade work, you may need full planning instead. But for many buildings, especially those with good natural light and sensible layouts, Class MA provides everything you need.

In simple terms, Class MA is the government's invitation to repurpose the commercial spaces that no longer serve their original purpose. It is a practical, predictable, and investor-friendly route that has reshaped the landscape of UK property. When you understand how it works, you unlock opportunities that most people walk past every day.

4.2 Prior Approval vs Full Planning

One of the most important decisions in any commercial-to-residential project is choosing the correct planning route. Many beginners assume Prior Approval is simply "planning lite," while full planning is a more complicated version of the same thing. In reality, they are two entirely different processes, each with its own logic, risks, timelines, and strategic advantages. Understanding the difference allows you to choose the route that gives your project the highest chance of success and avoid wasting months on the wrong path.

Prior Approval is the streamlined route used for Class MA conversions. It exists because the government has already approved the principle of turning Class E buildings into homes. That means the council cannot debate whether the building should remain commercial or whether the high street "needs" the shop. Their role is limited to assessing a small number of technical matters such as natural light, noise, transport impact, contamination, and flooding. If the building meets the criteria, the council must approve it. This makes Prior Approval predictable, faster, and far less political than full planning. The timeline reflects this simplicity. Councils have 56 days to make a decision. If they fail to respond in time, the application is deemed approved. Documentation is lighter too. You still need drawings, reports, and evidence, but the scope is narrower. You are not redesigning the building; you are demonstrating that the conversion meets the technical standards. For many investors, this speed and clarity make Prior Approval the preferred route.

Full planning is a different world. Here, the council has complete discretion. They can debate design, density, parking, character, heritage, and the impact on the local area. They can reject the application because they dislike the façade, the layout, or the loss of commercial space. They can ask for revisions, consultations, and additional reports. Full planning is slower, more political, and more subjective. A typical application takes 8–16 weeks, often longer once revisions and negotiations are factored in.

So why would anyone choose full planning? Because Prior Approval has limits. It does not allow you to extend the building, add floors, alter the external appearance significantly, or reconfigure the structure in ways that fall outside the conversion itself. If your vision requires architectural freedom new windows, balconies, extensions, roof alterations, or major structural changes, full planning becomes the correct route. It is also the better option when you want to maximize value through design rather than simply convert what already exists.

A few simple principles help guide the choice:

• Use Prior Approval when the building works as it is and you want speed, predictability, and minimal council interference.

• *Use full planning when you need design freedom, structural changes, or a more ambitious scheme.*

The smartest investors don't treat Prior Approval and full planning as competing routes. They treat them as tools each suited to a different type of building and a different type of opportunity. When you understand the strengths and limitations of both, you stop guessing and start strategizing. That clarity is what turns planning from a barrier into an advantage.

4.3 The Removal of the 1,500 sqm Limit and What It Means

For years, Class MA came with a ceiling: a hard limit of 1,500 square metres. Anything larger big offices, department stores, retail warehouses, multi-storey commercial blocks was automatically excluded from the permitted development route. Developers could still convert them, but only through full planning, which meant uncertainty, delays, and the risk of political objections. That size cap shaped the entire market. It kept PDR focused on small and medium-sized buildings and left the larger opportunities locked behind the gate of full planning.

That gate is now gone.

The removal of the 1,500 sqm limit is one of the most significant planning changes in recent years. It has quietly opened the door to a new category of projects buildings that were previously too large, too complex, or too politically sensitive to be considered under Class MA. Suddenly, the kinds of buildings that dominate town centres and high streets are eligible for Prior Approval. This shift has changed not just what is possible, but what is practical.

The most immediate impact is scale. Without the size restriction, developers can now consider multi-unit schemes that were previously off-limits. Large office blocks that once required full planning can now be converted under a streamlined process. Former department stores the giants of the high street can be repurposed into dozens of apartments without entering a political debate about "loss of retail."

Retail warehouses, sprawling commercial floors, and multi-storey Class E buildings suddenly become viable PDR candidates.

This change also alters the economics of conversion. Larger buildings often come with lower price-per-square-foot values because commercial demand for big units has collapsed in many towns. Under the old rules, these buildings were tempting but risky. Now, with Prior Approval available, the risk profile shifts dramatically. Developers can approach large assets with the confidence that the council cannot object to the principle of conversion. They can focus on technical compliance rather than political negotiation.

The removal of the limit also encourages more ambitious design thinking. When you are no longer constrained by size, you can explore layouts that include internal courtyards, co-living clusters, amenity spaces, or mixed-density configurations. Larger buildings offer deeper floor plates, multiple access points, and structural flexibility that smaller units simply cannot match. They allow for economies of scale in construction, professional fees, and long-term management.

Of course, scale brings its own challenges. Larger buildings require more detailed fire strategies, more complex service layouts, and more robust natural-light solutions. They may need internal reconfiguration to avoid deep, unusable zones. They also attract more scrutiny from councils, even under Prior Approval, because the impact on transport, noise, and local infrastructure is greater. But these challenges are technical, not political and technical challenges can be solved.

The real significance of removing the 1,500 sqm limit is this: Class MA is no longer a small-building tool. It is a town-centre regeneration tool. It allows investors to take on projects that reshape entire blocks, revive failing commercial zones, and deliver meaningful housing supply at scale. For developers with vision, this is the moment the market widened. The buildings that once felt out of reach are now firmly within the realm of possibility.

4.4 Local Nuances and Council Attitudes

Although planning law is national, planning culture is local. Two councils can read the same legislation and behave in completely different ways. One embraces Class MA as a tool for regeneration; another treats it as an inconvenience. One processes Prior Approval applications efficiently; another drags its feet, requests unnecessary clarifications, or interprets technical matters more aggressively than the next borough. Understanding these local nuances is one of the most underrated skills in commercial-to-residential development.

Every council has its own personality. Some are pragmatic, solution-focused, and quietly supportive of developers who bring investment into their area. Others are cautious, political, or protective of their commercial zones. Some councils are overwhelmed and slow simply because they lack staff. Others are slow because they are risk-averse and prefer to over-scrutinize applications. When you learn to read these behaviors early, you can adapt your strategy and avoid unnecessary frustration.

A council's attitude often reveals itself long before you submit anything. Their planning portal tells a story. If you see a steady stream of approved Class MA applications, it signals a council that understands the purpose of PDR and applies it fairly. If you see repeated refusals on technical grounds noise, transport, natural light it suggests a council that uses the limited Prior Approval criteria as a gatekeeping tool. Neither approach is illegal, but they create very different experiences for developers.

Local housing pressure also shapes behavior. Councils with acute housing shortages tend to be more open to residential conversions, even if they are not enthusiastic about losing commercial space. Councils with strong retail or employment protection policies may resist conversions more aggressively, even under PDR, by pushing technical objections to their limits. Understanding the local political climate helps you anticipate how your application will be received.

Sometimes the nuance is geographical. A council may be supportive of conversions in declining high streets but protective of prime commercial zones. They may welcome residential use in neighborhood centres but resist it in business parks. They may approve conversions in older buildings but push back on newer stock they believe still has commercial value. These patterns are rarely written in policy documents, but they are visible in past decisions.

A few subtle indicators help you read a council's attitude quickly:
- *A history of approving similar schemes in the same area*
- *The tone and clarity of their planning guidance*
- *The speed at which they process Prior Approval applications*

These clues don't guarantee an outcome, but they help you understand the environment you're stepping into. The smartest investors don't fight council culture they work with it. If a council is supportive, they move quickly and confidently. If a council is cautious, they prepare stronger reports, anticipate objections, and choose consultants who know the local quirks. If a council is openly resistant, they may choose a different building, a different area, or a different planning route altogether.

Local nuance is not a barrier; it is a map. When you learn to read it, you stop guessing and start strategizing and that is what turns planning from a gamble into a predictable process.

4.5 When Permitted Development Rights (PDR) Is Not the Right Route

Permitted Development Rights have transformed commercial-to-residential conversion, but they are not a universal solution. Many beginners assume PDR is always the fastest, safest, and most profitable route, simply because it avoids the politics of full planning. In reality, there are situations where PDR becomes a limitation rather than an advantage. Knowing when not to use PDR is just as important as knowing how to use it well. The most experienced developers don't force a building into Class MA; they choose the route that gives them the greatest control, flexibility, and long-term value.

The first scenario where PDR falls short is when the building needs external or structural changes. Class MA allows conversion, not redevelopment. If your vision requires new windows, balconies, extensions, roof alterations, or significant façade improvements, PDR will not give you the freedom you need. Full planning becomes the better route because it allows you to reshape the building rather than simply repurpose what already exists. This is especially true for deep-plan buildings where natural light is limited. Under PDR, you cannot add new openings freely; under full planning, you can design the building properly.

Another situation where PDR is not ideal is when the building sits in a sensitive location. Conservation areas, heritage zones, and areas with strong design controls often require a level of architectural consideration that PDR cannot accommodate. Even if Class MA technically applies, councils in these areas scrutinise applications more aggressively, using the limited Prior Approval criteria to push back. In these contexts, a well-designed full planning application can actually be smoother because it shows respect for the local character and gives the council something they can support.

There are also buildings where the commercial layout simply doesn't translate into good homes. PDR forces you to work within the existing envelope. If the floor plate is awkward, the circulation is poor, or the natural light is insufficient, you may end up with compromised units that are hard to sell or rent. Full planning allows you to reconfigure the structure, adjust the massing, or redesign the internal flow. Sometimes the best value comes not from squeezing units into a rigid shell, but from reshaping the building to create homes people genuinely want to live in.

A few subtle indicators help you recognize when PDR may not be the right route:

- *The building needs architectural freedom to reach its full value.*
- *The location demands a sensitive design response.*
- *The existing structure limits the quality of the final units.*

Finally, there are strategic reasons to avoid PDR. Some developers choose full planning because it creates a stronger planning history, increases the building's long-term value, or allows them to add floors and extensions that dramatically improve the GDV. PDR is fast, but full planning can be transformative. The key is simple: PDR is a tool, not a shortcut. When it aligns with the building, it is unbeatable. When it doesn't, the smartest move is to step back and choose the route that gives you the freedom to create something better.

Chapter 5: Building Regulations & Fire Safety

5.1 Overview of the Building Safety Act 2022

The Building Safety Act is one of the most significant shifts in UK construction and property regulation in decades. It didn't emerge in isolation. It was shaped by the aftermath of the Grenfell Tower fire in 2017, a tragedy that exposed deep structural failures in how buildings were designed, built, inspected, and managed. After years of inquiry, reform proposals, and industry consultation, the government introduced a new legal framework and in April 2022, the Building Safety Act officially became law.

For anyone involved in commercial-to-residential conversion, this Act is not background noise. It is the foundation that governs how your building must be designed, documented, and delivered. Even if your project is small, even if it falls under Permitted Development Rights, and even if you are not altering the external structure, the Act still shapes your responsibilities. It has changed the culture of building control, the expectations of regulators, and the accountability placed on developers.

At its core, the Building Safety Act introduces three major shifts that every investor must understand. The first is the creation of the Building Safety Regulator, a new body with real authority. Its role is to oversee building safety across the entire lifecycle of a building from design to construction to long-term management. Unlike previous systems, this regulator can investigate, enforce, and intervene. It is not a passive observer; it is an active guardian of safety standards.

The second shift is the introduction of duty holders. These are the individuals and organizations legally responsible for ensuring safety at every stage of a project. Developers, designers, contractors, and building owners all carry defined responsibilities. You cannot simply assume your architect will "handle compliance" or that your contractor will "sort out fire safety." The Act makes accountability explicit, traceable, and enforceable.

The third shift is the requirement for a "golden thread" of information a clear, accurate, and continuously updated record of how the building was designed, built, and maintained. While this requirement is most stringent for high-risk buildings, the cultural impact extends to all projects. Building control officers now expect clarity, evidence, and professionalism, even on smaller conversions. Vague drawings, incomplete specifications, and informal site decisions are no longer acceptable.

For commercial conversions, the Act matters even more because these projects often involve older buildings with unknown histories. You may inherit hidden defects, outdated materials, or structural quirks that were never documented. The Act forces you to confront these issues early. It pushes you to investigate, verify, and design with safety at the forefront rather than as an afterthought.

A few themes run through the Act:

- *Safety must be designed in, not inspected in.*
- *Accountability must be clear, not assumed.*
- *Information must be accurate, not approximate.*

The Building Safety Act is not about slowing developers down. It is about raising the standard of homes being created especially when those homes are carved out of buildings that were never intended for residential use. When you understand the Act, you don't just comply with the law; you build better, safer, more resilient homes.

5.2 Fire Safety Requirements in Conversions

Fire safety sits at the centre of every commercial-to-residential conversion. Long before you think about layouts, finishes, or interior design, you must understand how people will escape, how fire will be contained, and how the building will perform under stress. Commercial buildings were never designed for sleeping occupants, which means the moment you convert them into homes, the fire-safety expectations change dramatically. This is where many inexperienced developers get caught out. They assume fire safety is a box-ticking exercise, when in reality it shapes the entire design.

The first principle is simple: every flat must have a safe, protected route to escape. In a commercial building, circulation routes are often open, exposed, or visually appealing but they are rarely fire-resistant. When converting, you must create a protected corridor or staircase that can withstand fire long enough for residents to escape. This usually means fire-rated walls, fire-rated ceilings, and fire-rated doors forming a continuous, uncompromised route from each dwelling to the final exit. If the existing layout cannot support a protected route, the entire scheme may need rethinking.

Fire doors are another non-negotiable element. They are not decorative features; they are engineered components designed to hold back fire and smoke. In conversions, fire doors are required at key points: flat entrances, plant rooms, service cupboards, and along protected corridors. They must be correctly rated, correctly installed, and correctly certified. A single poorly fitted fire door can undermine the entire strategy.

Compartmentation is the backbone of fire safety in residential buildings. The idea is simple: if a fire starts in one flat, it must stay in that flat long enough for everyone else to escape. Commercial buildings often have large open spaces, suspended ceilings, or hidden voids that allow fire to spread rapidly. During conversion, these voids must be sealed, walls must be upgraded, and floors must be reinforced to create proper fire-resistant compartments. This is one of the most common areas where developers underestimate cost and complexity.

Alarms and detection systems also change when a building becomes residential. Commercial alarms are designed for daytime occupancy and staff response. Residential alarms must protect sleeping occupants. Most conversions require an integrated fire-detection system, often a Grade A or Grade D system depending on the scale and layout. The system must be designed so that residents are alerted early, even if the fire starts in a different part of the building.

Sprinklers are not mandatory in every conversion, but they become essential in certain scenarios for example, when escape routes are compromised, when layouts are tight, or when the building exceeds certain height thresholds. Sprinklers can also unlock design flexibility, allowing layouts that would otherwise be impossible under standard fire-safety rules.

Because every building is different, the role of a fire engineer becomes crucial. A competent fire engineer doesn't just check compliance; they shape the strategy. They analyze the building's structure, materials, escape routes, and risk profile. They help you design a solution that is safe, compliant, and buildable. In many conversions, the fire engineer's input is what turns a marginal scheme into a viable one.

Fire safety is not an afterthought. It is the framework that determines what you can build, how you can build it, and whether the building will ever be signed off. When you understand fire safety early, you avoid redesigns, delays, and costly surprises and you create homes that genuinely protect the people who live in them.

5.3 Energy Performance Certificate (EPC) Targets and Energy Performance

Energy performance has quietly become one of the most important factors in commercial-to-residential conversion. For years, EPC ratings were treated as an administrative formality as a certificate you needed at the end of the project. Today, they shape design decisions from the very beginning. With the UK moving toward stricter energy-efficiency standards, developers can no longer afford to treat EPCs as an afterthought. A building that cannot reach the required rating risks becoming unmortgageable, unlettable, or non-compliant with future regulations.

The first thing to understand is that EPC ratings are not just about insulation. They reflect the entire energy profile of a home, how it retains heat, how it generates heat, how it is ventilated, and how efficiently it uses energy. Commercial buildings often start from a disadvantage. Many have large single-glazed shopfronts, uninsulated walls, ageing ***Heating, Ventilation and Air Conditioning (HVAC)*** systems, or thermal bridges that leak heat. When converting, you must bring the building up to modern residential standards, which often requires more intervention than people expect.

Insulation is the foundation. Walls, floors, and roofs must meet minimum U-values, and in older commercial buildings, this often means adding internal insulation, external insulation, or both. Each option affects space, cost, and design. Internal insulation reduces room sizes; external insulation changes the façade. Neither choice is trivial. But without proper insulation, achieving a strong EPC rating becomes nearly impossible.

Windows are another major factor. Many commercial units have large panes of glass designed for display, not thermal performance. Replacing them with high-performance double or triple glazing is often essential. This improves energy efficiency but also affects acoustics, security, and aesthetics. In some cases, especially in conservation areas, window upgrades require careful negotiation with planning officers.

Heating systems are where many conversions succeed or fail. Gas boilers are still allowed, but the direction of travel is clear: the UK is moving toward low-carbon heating. Heat pumps, electric panel heaters, and hybrid systems are becoming more common, especially in smaller units. The choice of heating system has a direct impact on the EPC rating. A poorly chosen system can drag a property down to a D or E rating, while a well-designed electric system can lift it to a B.

Ventilation also plays a critical role. Modern insulation creates airtight homes, which means you must manage airflow properly. Mechanical ventilation with heat recovery (MVHR) is becoming increasingly common in conversions because it improves air quality while retaining heat. It also boosts EPC performance by reducing energy loss.

A few key principles help guide energy-performance decisions:

- *Insulation and airtightness must be planned early, not retrofitted.*
- *Heating systems must align with future regulations, not just current ones.*
- *Windows and ventilation must work together to balance efficiency and comfort.*

Future-proofing is essential. Regulations are tightening, lenders are becoming more selective, and tenants increasingly expect energy-efficient homes. A conversion that only just meets today's standards may fall behind within a few years. A conversion that exceeds them will remain valuable, compliant, and attractive long into the future.

Energy performance is not just a regulatory requirement it is a competitive advantage. When you design with EPC targets in mind from day one, you create homes that are cheaper to run, easier to finance, and more resilient to the changes ahead.

5.4 Soundproofing, Insulation, and Modern Standards

When you convert a commercial building into homes, you are not just changing its use you are changing the way it must perform. A shop, office, or café can tolerate noise transfer, heat loss, and lightweight partitions. A home cannot. Residential standards demand comfort, privacy, warmth, and acoustic separation that commercial buildings were never designed to provide. This is why soundproofing, insulation, and building-fabric upgrades sit at the heart of every successful conversion. They are not optional extras; they are the difference between a compliant home and a building control failure.

Two key regulations shape this part of the process: Approved Document E (soundproofing) and Approved Document L (energy performance). These documents set the minimum standards for acoustic separation, thermal insulation, and overall building efficiency. Meeting them is essential. Exceeding them is what creates homes people genuinely want to live in.

Soundproofing begins with understanding how noise travels. Commercial buildings often have open floor plates, suspended ceilings, and lightweight partitions that allow sound to move freely between spaces. In a residential setting, this is unacceptable. You must create proper separating walls and floors that block airborne noise (voices, music, televisions) and impact noise (footsteps, movement, vibrations). This usually requires dense materials, resilient layers, acoustic insulation, and carefully detailed junctions. A single gap or poorly sealed joint can undermine the entire system.

Floors are especially challenging. Many commercial buildings have timber floors or hollow voids that amplify sound. To meet the standards in Approved Document E, you may need to add acoustic mats, floating floors, or resilient bars. These upgrades add cost and thickness, which affects ceiling heights a detail many developers overlook until late in the design process. Good acoustic design must be planned early, not retrofitted.

Thermal insulation is governed by Approved Document L, which focuses on reducing heat loss and improving energy efficiency. Commercial buildings often have uninsulated walls, thin roofs, and large areas of glazing. To meet modern residential standards, you must upgrade the building fabric significantly. This may involve internal wall insulation, external wall insulation, roof insulation, or a combination of all three. Each choice affects space, appearance, and cost. Internal insulation reduces room sizes; external insulation changes the façade. Neither option is trivial, but both are essential for achieving strong Energy Performance Certificate (EPC) ratings.

Modern standards also require airtightness and the ability of a building to prevent uncontrolled drafts. When you improve airtightness, you must also improve ventilation. Mechanical ventilation systems, especially mechanical ventilation with heat recovery (MVHR), are becoming common in conversions because they maintain air quality while retaining heat. This improves comfort and energy performance simultaneously.

A few guiding principles help developers navigate this stage:

- *Acoustic and thermal upgrades must be designed early, not added at the end.*
- *Separating floors and walls must be robust enough to meet testing requirements.*
- *Insulation, airtightness, and ventilation must work together as a system.*

When you approach soundproofing and insulation with intention, you create homes that feel solid, warm, private, and modern the kind of homes that stand out in the market and pass building control with confidence.

5.5 Working with Building Control

Building control is the quiet force that determines whether your commercial-to-residential conversion becomes a legally habitable home. You can have the perfect layout, the right planning route, and a strong construction team, but if building control is not satisfied, the project cannot be signed off. Many new developers misunderstand this relationship. They treat building control as an obstacle or a final hurdle. In reality, building control is a partner one whose involvement should begin early and continue throughout the entire build.

The first thing to understand is the role of the building control officer. Their job is to ensure that your conversion meets the technical standards set out in the Building Regulations. These regulations cover everything from fire safety to structure, soundproofing, ventilation, drainage, insulation, and accessibility. Building control officers do not care about aesthetics or design preferences. They care about safety, performance, and compliance. Their responsibility is to protect future residents, not to make your life difficult.

You have two options for building control: the local authority building control service or an approved inspector (a private building control professional). Both perform the same function, but they differ in approach. Local authorities tend to be more formal, more procedural, and sometimes slower due to workload. Approved inspectors are often more collaborative, more responsive, and more commercially minded. Neither option is "better" the right choice depends on the complexity of your project and the level of support you need.

The inspection process begins long before anyone steps on site. You must submit detailed plans, specifications, and supporting documents. These include fire strategies, structural calculations, acoustic details, insulation specifications, and mechanical and electrical layouts. The clearer and more complete your documentation, the smoother the approval process will be. Building control officers do not like surprises. They want to see that you understand the regulations and have designed the building accordingly.

Once construction begins, building control will visit the site at key stages. These inspections are not optional. They ensure that what is being built matches what was approved. Typical inspection points include foundations (if altered), structural works, fire-stopping, insulation installation, drainage, and final completion. If something is wrong, building control will require it to be corrected and they will not sign off the project until it is.

A few principles make the process smoother:

• *Involve building control early, not halfway through construction.*
• *Provide clear, complete documentation ambiguity creates delays.*
• *Keep communication open; building control officers appreciate transparency.*

The most successful developers treat building control as a collaborator. They ask questions early, share drawings proactively, and welcome inspections rather than fear them. When building control feels respected and informed, the entire process becomes smoother, faster, and far less stressful.

Working with building control is not about passing an exam at the end. It is about building a safe, compliant, high-quality home from the beginning. When you understand their role and integrate them into your process, you avoid costly rework, protect your timeline, and deliver a building that stands up to scrutiny both legally and professionally.

Chapter 6: Navigating Article 4 Directions

6.1 What Article 4 Is and Why It Matters

Article 4 Directions are one of the most misunderstood parts of the planning system, yet they have a huge impact on commercial-to-residential conversions. Many new developers hear the term and assume it is a blanket ban or a hostile planning tool. In reality, Article 4 is simply a mechanism that allows councils to remove certain Permitted Development Rights (PDR) in specific areas. It does not change national law. It does not rewrite planning policy. It simply means that, in certain locations, you must apply for full planning permission instead of relying on PDR.

To understand why Article 4 matters, you first need to understand its purpose. Permitted Development Rights were created to speed up development and reduce pressure on the planning system. They allow certain changes of use such as converting Class E buildings into homes under Class MA without needing full planning permission. But PDR is a national tool, and not every area benefits from unrestricted conversions. Some high streets are fragile. Some employment zones are strategically important. Some conservation areas require careful control. Article 4 gives councils the ability to protect these areas by removing specific PDR routes. When a council issues Article 4 Direction, it is not banning development. It is simply saying:

"In this location, we want full oversight. You must apply for full planning permission."

This distinction is crucial. Article 4 does not stop you from converting a building. It just changes the route you must take. Many developers wrongly assume that Article 4 areas are off-limits. In reality, some of the best opportunities exist in Article 4 zones especially where councils still support residential development but want to control design quality.

Councils typically use Article 4 Directions for three reasons:
a. To protect employment land especially offices, industrial estates, and business parks.
b. To preserve key commercial centres where losing shops or services would harm the local economy.
c. To maintain character in sensitive areas such as conservation zones or heritage districts.

For commercial-to-residential developers, the impact is strategic. If a building sits inside an Article 4 area, you cannot rely on Class MA. You must submit a full planning application, which means design scrutiny, public consultation, and a longer timeline. But it also means greater design freedom. You can add windows, extend the building, alter the façade, or reconfigure the structure things PDR would not allow.

The smartest investors do not avoid Article 4 areas. They study them. They understand why the council applied the restriction and what types of development the council still supports. In some towns, Article 4 applies only to ground-floor commercial units, leaving upper floors free for conversion. In others, Article 4 applies only to specific streets, not entire districts. These nuances create opportunities that less informed developers miss.

Article 4 is not a barrier, it is a signal. It tells you where councils want control, where they want quality, and where they want thoughtful development rather than automatic conversions. When you understand Article 4, you stop fearing it and start using it to your advantage.

6.2 How to Check If an Area Is Restricted

Before you commit to a commercial-to-residential conversion, you must know whether the building sits inside an Article 4 Direction zone. This is not something you can guess, assume, or rely on hearsay for. Article 4 boundaries can be extremely precise sometimes covering a single street, a cluster of shops, or even one side of a road but not the other. Missing this detail can derail your entire strategy. Fortunately, checking whether an area is restricted is straightforward once you know where to look and how to interpret the information.

The first and most reliable source is the local council's planning website. Every council that has issued Article 4 Direction must publish the details publicly. This usually includes a written notice, a map, and a description of the affected area. Some councils provide interactive maps; others provide PDF documents that require careful reading. The key is not to skim. Article 4 boundaries often follow unusual lines of property edges, rear boundaries, or historic zoning borders. A building may appear outside the zone at first glance but fall inside once you examine the map closely.

The second place to check is the council's Local Plan or planning policy documents. These documents explain why Article 4 Direction exists and what the council is trying to protect. Understanding the reasoning helps you anticipate how the council will treat applications in the area. For example, if the Article 4 Direction is designed to protect employment land, the council may resist residential conversions but support mixed-use schemes. If it is designed to preserve a high street, they may allow upper-floor conversions but restrict ground-floor changes. Policy context matters.

The third tool is the planning portal specifically, the planning history of the building and nearby properties. If you see repeated refusals for Class MA applications in the area, that is a strong indicator that an Article 4 Direction is in place. Conversely, if you see successful conversions nearby, it may mean the building sits outside the restricted zone. Planning history is not definitive, but it provides valuable clues.

Cross-checking is essential. Never rely on a single source. A council map may be outdated. A PDF may be unclear. A planning officer may give you verbal guidance that is incomplete.

The safest approach is to check:

- *The Article 4 map*
- *The written Article 4 notice*
- *The Local Plan*
- *The planning history of the building*
- *The council's interactive GIS map (if available)*

If all sources align, you can proceed with confidence. If anything is unclear, request written confirmation from the council. Do not rely on phone calls or informal conversations. Written confirmation protects you if a dispute arises later.

The smartest investors treat Article 4 checks as part of their due-diligence routine. They verify boundaries before offering on a building, not after. They understand that a single street can contain both restricted and unrestricted properties. They know that Article 4 is not a deal-breaker it simply changes the planning route.

When you learn to check Article 4 boundaries properly, you eliminate guesswork, avoid costly surprises, and position yourself to make informed, strategic decisions in every market.

6.3 Common Article 4 Patterns in UK Towns and Cities

Article 4 Directions may look random to beginners, but they are anything but. Councils apply them with purpose, usually to protect areas they consider strategically important. Once you understand the patterns, you can walk through a town centre and predict with surprising accuracy where Article 4 is likely to appear. This knowledge gives you an edge. It helps you avoid wasted time; spot overlooked opportunities and understand the political logic behind local planning decisions.

The most common pattern is the protection of high-value commercial centres. Councils rely on business rates, footfall, and economic activity from their core retail zones. If too many shops convert into flats, the high street weakens. To prevent this, councils often apply Article 4 Directions to the main shopping streets, town squares, and primary commercial corridors. These areas are considered essential to the local economy, so councils want full control over any change of use. This does not mean residential is unwelcome, it simply means the council wants to assess each proposal individually.

The second major pattern is employment zones. Business parks, office districts, industrial estates, and strategic employment areas are often protected by Article 4. Councils fear that unrestricted conversions could hollow out their employment base, reduce job opportunities, and undermine long-term economic plans. In these areas, Article 4 is used as a defensive tool. Councils want to ensure that any loss of employment space is justified, balanced, and aligned with their economic strategy. For developers, this means that large office-to-residential conversions may require full planning, even if the building would otherwise qualify under Permitted Development Rights (PDR).

Another common pattern is conservation areas and heritage districts. These areas are protected for their architectural, cultural, or historical value. Councils use Article 4 to prevent uncontrolled changes that could damage the character of the area. This often includes restrictions on shopfronts, façades, and changes of use. In these locations, councils want to ensure that any conversion respects the heritage context. Interestingly, some councils allow upper-floor conversions even in conservation areas, while restricting ground-floor changes. This creates opportunities for developers who understand the nuance.

A fourth pattern is transport hubs and regeneration zones. Areas around major stations, new transport links, or planned regeneration projects often receive Article 4 protection. Councils want to shape development in these zones carefully because they expect long-term growth. They may support residential use, but they want to control density, design, and the mix of uses. Article 4 gives them the oversight they need to guide the area's evolution.

A few consistent themes emerge across the country:

- *Councils protect areas that are economically or historically important.*
- *Article 4 is used to manage change, not to stop development.*
- *Restrictions often apply to ground floors but not upper floors.*
- *Boundaries are precise sometimes down to a single block.*

When you recognize these patterns, you stop seeing Article 4 as a barrier and start seeing it as a predictable part of the planning landscape. You learn where councils want control, where they want quality, and where they want thoughtful development rather than automatic conversions. And that insight gives you a strategic advantage in every town and city you explore.

6.4 Adapting Your Strategy in Article 4 Zones

Operating in an Article 4 Direction zone does not mean opportunity disappears it simply means the rules of the game change. Many inexperienced developers panic when they discover a building sit inside an Article 4 area, assuming the project is no longer viable. In reality, some of the most profitable and high-quality schemes in the UK sit within Article 4 boundaries. The key is knowing how to adapt your strategy, strengthen your approach, and work with the council's expectations rather than against them.

The first shift is mindset. Article 4 does not ban development; it removes Permitted Development Rights (PDR) and requires you to apply for full planning permission. This means more scrutiny, more documentation, and more design work but it also gives you more freedom. Under full planning, you can add windows, alter façades, extend the building, or reconfigure the structure in ways that PDR would never allow. In many cases, full planning unlocks value that a simple Class MA conversion could not.

The second shift is understanding what the council is trying to protect. Article 4 Directions are never random. They are applied to safeguard employment zones, heritage areas, high-value commercial centres, or strategic regeneration sites. When you understand the council's motivation, you can shape your proposal to align with their priorities. For example, if the Article 4 Direction protects employment land, a mixed-use scheme that retains ground-floor commercial space may be more successful than a pure residential conversion. If the Direction protects a heritage area, a sensitive design that enhances the façade may win support.

The third shift is strengthening your planning application. In Article 4 zones, you cannot rely on the automatic fallback of PDR. You must demonstrate that your proposal is well-designed, policy-compliant, and beneficial to the area.

This means investing in:

- *A strong planning statement*
- *High-quality architectural drawings*

• *A heritage or design-impact assessment (if relevant)*
• *A clear justification for the loss of commercial space*
• *Evidence of market demand for residential use*

Councils respond well to professionalism. A well-prepared application signals that you understand the area, respect the policy context, and are committed to delivering quality.

The fourth shift is identifying viable opportunities despite restrictions. Article 4 zones often contain overlooked gems upper floors above shops, redundant office suites, or underused commercial buildings that councils are willing to see repurposed if the design is right. Many councils apply Article 4 only to ground-floor use, leaving upper floors free for conversion. Others allow residential use if the proposal enhances the streetscape or supports regeneration goals. The key is reading the nuance rather than assuming the entire zone is off-limits.

Finally, the most successful developers build relationships. Pre-application discussions, early engagement with planning officers, and clear communication can transform the process. When a council sees that you understand their priorities and are willing to work collaboratively, they are far more likely to support your proposal.

Adapting your strategy in an Article 4 zone is not about avoiding restrictions it is about navigating them intelligently. When you understand the purpose behind the policy and align your design with local priorities, you turn Article 4 from a barrier into a strategic advantage.

6.5 When Full Planning May Still Work

Many developers assume that once a building sits inside an Article 4 Direction zone, the door to residential conversion is effectively closed. This is one of the biggest misconceptions in the industry. Article 4 does not ban development. It simply removes Permitted Development Rights (PDR) and requires you to go through the full planning process. And while full planning is more detailed and more scrutinized, it can absolutely succeed sometimes more easily than people expect.

The key is understanding why the council applied Article 4 Direction in the first place. Councils do not use Article 4 randomly. They use it to protect specific interests: employment land, heritage character, high-value commercial centres, or strategic regeneration zones. When your proposal aligns with those interests or enhances them full planning becomes not only possible but often welcome.

One of the strongest routes to success is a high-quality design proposal. Councils in Article 4 areas are not opposed to residential use; they are opposed to uncontrolled, low-quality conversions. When you present a thoughtful design that improves the building, enhances the streetscape, and respects local character, you stand out immediately. High-quality architecture, sensitive materials, and well-considered layouts can turn a skeptical planning officer into a supporter.

Another powerful argument is local housing need. Every council in the UK faces pressure to deliver more homes. If you can demonstrate that your proposal helps meet that need, especially for smaller units, accessible homes, or affordable housing, you strengthen your case. Planning officers respond well to evidence-based arguments. A clear housing-needs assessment or reference to the council's own policy documents can shift the conversation in your favor.

Full planning also works well when the building itself aligns with regeneration goals. Many Article 4 zones sit within areas undergoing transformation new transport links, town-centre renewal, or mixed-use redevelopment. Councils often want residential use in these areas, but they want it delivered in a controlled, high-quality way. If your proposal supports regeneration by activating a dead frontage, improving a neglected building, or bringing life back to an underused block the council may view it as a positive contribution. There are also practical scenarios where full planning is the better route even without Article 4.

For example:

- *When the building needs new windows or façade improvements*
- *When extensions or roof alterations are required*
- *When the existing layout is unsuitable for PDR-style conversion*
- *When the site offers potential for additional floors or massing*

In these cases, full planning gives you the design freedom to unlock value that PDR would restrict.

The most successful developers treat Article 4 as a signal, not a stop sign. They study the policy context, understand the council's priorities, and shape their proposals accordingly. They invest in strong planning statements, heritage assessments, and design rationales. They engage early with planning officers and demonstrate that their scheme is not just compliant but beneficial.

Full planning inside an Article 4 zone is not a battle it is a negotiation. When you align your proposal with the council's goals, you turn Article 4 from a barrier into a strategic advantage.

Part 3: Design & Analysis

Part 3 marks a turning point in this book. Up to now, we've focused on understanding the rules, the planning landscape, and the regulatory framework that shapes commercial-to-residential conversions. But knowledge alone doesn't create profitable projects. What separates successful developers from everyone else is their ability to analyze a building intelligently and design a layout that works in the real world. This part of the book is where strategy becomes practical. It's where you learn to look at a building and see not just what it is, but what it could become.

Commercial-to-residential conversion is not guesswork. It is discipline. Every profitable scheme begins long before architects draw their first line. It begins with analysis of a structured, methodical way of assessing whether a building is viable, what constraints it carries, and how much value you can unlock. Many beginners rush into design too quickly. They fall in love with a building, assume it will convert easily, and only later discover the hidden issues that destroy the numbers. Part 3 teaches you how to avoid that trap. It gives you the tools to evaluate a building with clarity, confidence, and professional discipline.

Chapter 7 focuses on how to analyze a commercial conversion deal. This is the foundation of everything that follows. You will learn how to read a building like an experienced developer understanding its structure, its layout, its services, its constraints, and its potential. You will learn how to identify red flags early, how to estimate what is realistically achievable, and how to determine whether the building can support the number of units you need for the deal to work. This chapter shows you how to combine planning knowledge, building regulations, fire safety, and market demand into a single, coherent analysis. By the end of it, you will know how to walk into any commercial building and assess its viability with a level of confidence that most investors never reach.

But analysis alone is not enough. Once you understand what the building can support, you must design a layout that is both compliant and commercially strong. That is the focus of Chapter 8 designing the residential layout. This chapter takes you inside the design process, showing you how to create homes that feel natural, functional, and desirable. You will learn how to position kitchens and bathrooms, how to maximize natural light, how to create efficient circulation, and how to avoid the common design mistakes that lead to awkward, unmarketable units. You will also learn how to design with building regulations in mind from the beginning, so you avoid costly redesigning later.

Part 3 bridges the gap between theory and execution. It shows you how to think like a developer, someone who balances creativity with compliance, ambition with practicality, and design with financial reality. You will learn how to make decisions that are grounded in evidence, not emotion. You will learn how to shape a building in a way that respects its constraints while unlocking its potential. And you will learn how to design homes that people genuinely want to live in, not just units that look good on paper.

This part of the book is about mastery. It is about developing analytical and design skills that allow you to move through the world of commercial conversions with confidence. When you understand how to analyze a building and design a layout that works, you stop guessing and start leading. You stop reacting to problems and start anticipating them. You stop hoping a deal will work and start knowing it will.

Part 3 gives you the tools to see opportunities where others see obstacles and to turn that opportunity into a profitable, compliant, beautifully designed reality.

Chapter 7: How to Analyse a Commercial Conversion Deal

Commercial conversions are won or lost before you ever exchange contracts. The analysis stage is where you separate a profitable opportunity from a financial trap. Unlike residential property, commercial buildings come with structural, legal, planning, and financial complexities that must be understood from day one.
This chapter gives you a step-by-step framework for analyzing any commercial-to-residential conversion with confidence.

a. Structural Integrity: The Foundation of Your Deal
Before you think about layouts, planning routes, or financial modelling, you must confirm that the building is structurally sound. Everything in a commercial-to-residential conversion depends on the integrity of the existing structure. If the building cannot safely support the new layout, the entire deal collapses or worse, the costs spiral far beyond what the numbers can sustain. Structural due diligence is not a formality; it is the foundation of your decision-making.
The first step is understanding how the building currently stands and how it will behave once converted. Commercial buildings often contain hidden weaknesses: outdated materials, unsupported spans, compromised beams, or historic movement that only becomes obvious once work begins. Identifying these issues early protects your budget and prevents costly redesigns.

Key structural checks include:
• Load-bearing walls and whether they can be safely removed or altered
• The condition and sizing of steel beams, especially in older or extended buildings
• Roof structure, including timber integrity, sagging, or historic repairs
• Evidence of subsidence, settlement, or structural movement
• Cracks in walls, ceilings, or floors that indicate deeper issues

• *Damp, rot, or water ingress that may have weakened structural elements*
• *Existing fire-escape routes and the structural fire protection supporting them*

A professional structural engineer's report is non-negotiable. No amount of experience, intuition, or visual inspection can replace the calculations, testing, and analysis that a qualified engineer provides. Their assessment determines what can be removed, what must be reinforced, and what additional steelwork or structural upgrades will be required to meet modern residential standards.

If the structure is compromised, your costs can escalate dramatically sometimes to the point where the deal is no longer viable. By confirming structural integrity at the very beginning, you protect your budget, your timeline, and your ability to deliver a safe, compliant, and profitable conversion.

b. Natural Light Compliance (The Silent Deal-Breaker)

Natural light is one of the most underestimated factors in commercial-to-residential conversion, yet it is one of the most decisive. Under Prior Approval rules, every habitable room must receive adequate natural light. This requirement is strict, measurable, and non-negotiable. No planning consultant, architect, or clever argument can override a room that fails the natural-light test. If the building cannot deliver compliant daylight levels, the deal may be fundamentally unviable.

The challenge is that many commercial buildings were never designed for residential use. Deep floor plates, limited windows, long internal corridors, and large open retail spaces often create areas that simply cannot receive enough daylight to qualify as habitable rooms. Identifying this early protects you from pursuing a scheme that will fail at the Prior Approval stage.

Your assessment must begin with the basics:

• *Window size; Are the existing openings large enough to illuminate the intended rooms?*
•*Window placement; Are windows positioned in a way that allows light*

to penetrate the space effectively?
• *Depth of the floor plate; How far does natural light travel before the room becomes too dark to qualify?*
• *Internal rooms; Are you trying to create bedrooms or living spaces without windows? If so, the scheme will fail.*
• *Potential for new openings; Can you add new windows, light wells, or rooflights? And if so, will planning allow it?*

These checks determine whether the building can support compliant, marketable homes. If the answer is no, the deal is not a deal it is a liability. Natural light is not just a regulatory requirement; it is a design truth. Homes without daylight feel oppressive, perform poorly, and fail both planning and market expectations. By assessing natural light at the very beginning, you avoid wasted time, protect your investment, and ensure your scheme has a genuine path to approval.

c. Floor-to-Ceiling Height: The Hidden Value Indicator

Floor-to-ceiling height is one of the most overlooked elements in commercial-to-residential analysis, yet it has a profound impact on design quality, compliance, and long-term value. Many beginners focus on square footage and forget that volume the height of the space is just as important. A room with generous height feels brighter, larger, and more comfortable, even if the floor area is modest. Conversely, a low ceiling can make an otherwise good layout feel cramped and unappealing.

The ideal residential height typically sits between 2.4 metres and 2.6 metres. This range provides enough space for comfortable living, effective lighting, and modern ventilation systems. The minimum acceptable height is usually around 2.3 metres, but anything close to the minimum requires careful design to avoid creating oppressive or unattractive rooms.

Low ceilings limit your options in several ways:

• *Layout flexibility; You may struggle to position kitchens, bathrooms, or mezzanines without the space feeling tight.*
• *Ventilation routes; Mechanical systems, ducting, and extract runs require vertical clearance.*

• *Fire-safety solutions; Fire-rated ceilings, sprinkler systems, and compartmentation often reduce usable height further.*
• *Market appeal; Tenants and buyers instinctively prefer taller, airier rooms.*

High ceilings, on the other hand, create a sense of luxury and spaciousness. They increase perceived room size, improve natural light distribution, and allow for more creative design solutions. In rental markets, higher ceilings often translate into stronger demand and higher achievable rents. In sales markets, they elevate the overall feel of the property and differentiate your units from competing stock. Ceiling height is not just a design detail it is a value indicator. By assessing it early, you avoid schemes that feel compromised and prioritize buildings that offer the space, comfort, and flexibility needed to create genuinely desirable homes.

d. Utilities & Services: The Lifeblood of the Building

Utilities and services are the hidden infrastructure that determines whether a commercial-to-residential conversion is practical, compliant, and financially viable. Many beginners focus on layouts and planning potential but overlook the essential systems that make a home functional. When these systems are inadequate, outdated, or poorly located, the cost of upgrading them can destroy the profitability of a deal. Understanding the building's service capacity early is not optional it is fundamental.

The first priority is drainage capacity, especially in multi-unit schemes. Commercial buildings often have limited drainage points designed for a single use, not multiple kitchens and bathrooms. If the existing system cannot support the number of proposed units, you may need new soil stacks, pumped systems, or extensive re-routing all of which add cost and complexity.

Next is water pressure. Residential units require consistent, reliable pressure for showers, appliances, and daily use. Older commercial buildings may have insufficient supply, requiring upgrades to incoming mains or internal distribution. Electrical capacity is another major factor. You must confirm whether the building has enough power for multiple residential units and whether three-phase electricity is required. Modern heating systems, induction hobs, and mechanical ventilation all increase electrical demand. Underestimating this can lead to expensive rewiring or supply upgrades.

You must also assess the gas supply or decide whether an all-electricity scheme is more realistic. Many developers now favor electric heating for simplicity and future-proofing, but this increases the importance of electrical capacity and ventilation design.

Other essential checks include:

- *Ventilation routes for kitchens and bathrooms*
- *Heating options and compatibility with the building's structure*
- *The condition and layout of existing service risers*

Most commercial buildings require full re-plumbing and rewiring. This is normal but failing to budget for it is one of the most common and costly mistakes developers make.

By assessing utilities early, you protect your budget, avoid surprises, and ensure your design is grounded in practical reality.

e. Roof Load Capacity: Can the Building Support More?

When analyzing a commercial-to-residential conversion, one of the most powerful values-add opportunities is the potential to build upwards or introduce new internal levels. But none of this is possible unless the existing roof and supporting structure can safely carry the additional load. Roof-load capacity is not a guess, an assumption, or something you "figure out later." It is a structural reality that determines whether your expansion plans are viable or financially dangerous. Any proposal that increases weight on the building must be assessed professionally.

This includes plans to:

- *Add a mezzanine level*
- *Add a new storey*
- *Convert the loft into habitable space*
- *Install heavy mechanical plant or HVAC equipment*

Each of these interventions introduces significant additional load. Commercial roofs vary widely in strength. Some are designed only to support lightweight coverings and minimal maintenance access. Others, especially older timber roofs, may already be weakened by age, water ingress, or historic alterations. Without proper analysis, you risk committing to a design that the structure simply cannot support.

A structural engineer will calculate the building's load-bearing capacity, assess the condition of the roof trusses, beams, and supporting walls, and determine whether reinforcement is required. This assessment is essential. Reinforcement is possible steel beams, strengthened joists, new supports, or even partial reconstruction but it must be priced into your appraisal from the beginning. Many deals fail because developers assume they can add floors cheaply, only to discover that the structural upgrades cost more than the uplift in value.

Roof-load capacity is not just a technical detail; it is a strategic filter. Buildings that can support additional massing often deliver exceptional returns. Buildings that cannot still work but only if you understand the limitations early and design within them. By confirming roof-load capacity at the start, you protect your budget, avoid unrealistic assumptions, and ensure your scheme is grounded in structural reality.

f. Noise, Contamination & Environmental Risks

Environmental risks are often invisible during the first viewing, yet they can have a profound impact on planning success, build cost, and long-term value. Many commercial buildings sit in locations shaped by decades of industrial use, heavy traffic, or historic contamination. If you fail to assess these risks early, you may commit to a deal that becomes financially or legally unworkable once the true conditions emerge.

One of the most common issues is noise. Buildings located near busy roads, rail lines, night-time venues, or industrial operations may require enhanced acoustic protection. Under residential standards, you must demonstrate that internal noise levels can be reduced to acceptable limits. This often means upgraded glazing, acoustic insulation, or mechanical ventilation, all of which add cost. If the noise environment is extreme, the council may resist residential use altogether.

Another major factor is contaminated land. Older commercial or industrial sites may contain pollutants in the soil or groundwater. This is especially common in former workshops, garages, factories, and sites with long industrial histories. Contamination does not automatically stop development, but it does require investigation, remediation, and sometimes specialist disposal, all of which must be priced into your appraisal. You must also consider flood risk. Buildings in flood zones face stricter planning requirements, potential insurance challenges, and design constraints such as raised floor levels or flood-resilient materials. Flood risk can be managed, but it must be understood early.

Other environmental concerns include:

- *Nearby industrial uses that generate odor, vibration, or operational disturbance*
- *Air-quality issues in dense urban areas*
- *Proximity to waste facilities, substations, or heavy-goods routes*

For older or industrial sites, a Phase 1 Environmental Report is a wise and often essential step. It identifies risks early, protects your budget, and ensures your scheme is grounded in environmental reality.

g. Space Standards & Layout Potential

Space standards are one of the most decisive factors in commercial-to-residential analysis because they directly determine how many units you can create and therefore how profitable the scheme can be. A building may look spacious at first glance, but once you apply minimum room sizes, corridor widths, escape distances, and storage requirements, the number of viable units can shrink dramatically. Understanding these constraints early allows you to design intelligently and avoid unrealistic assumptions.

The first step is confirming that your proposed units meet minimum space standards. Even when converting under Prior Approval routes, most councils expect layouts that align with national space guidance. Undersized studios, cramped bedrooms, or awkward living spaces may pass on paper but fail in practice either at planning stage or in the market.

Next, you must assess corridor widths and escape distances. Residential layouts must allow safe evacuation in the event of a fire, and this often dictates how far a unit can be from a protected staircase or exit. Long, narrow commercial floor plates can become problematic if escape distances exceed allowable limits. This can reduce the number of units or force you to introduce additional fire-safety measures.

You must also plan for bin and cycle storage, which are mandatory in most residential schemes. These spaces take up valuable floor area and must be positioned logically, often at ground level. Many beginners forget to allocate space for them, only to discover later that their layout no longer works.

Other essential checks include:

- *Ventilation and natural light for all habitable rooms*
- *Accessibility requirements for certain unit types*
- *Logical circulation that avoids wasted space*

Space standards are not just regulatory hurdles they are commercial realities. They determine how efficiently you can divide the building, how attractive the units will be, and ultimately whether the numbers stack.

h. Planning Constraints & Article 4

Planning constraints are one of the most decisive factors in commercial-to-residential conversions. A building can look perfect on paper great location, strong layout potential, and solid structure yet still fail as a deal if planning restrictions block your intended use. Before you commit to a purchase, you must confirm exactly what planning route is available and whether any local policies limit what you can achieve. This is not something to check after the offer; it is a core part of your early-stage due diligence.

The first question is whether the building qualifies for Class MA under Permitted Development Rights. Not every commercial building is eligible. Some fall outside Use Class E, some exceed the size limits, and others fail on vacancy requirements or natural-light rules. If the building cannot use Class MA, you must rely on full planning which is still possible but requires a different strategy and timeline.

Next, you must confirm whether the building sits inside an Article 4

Direction area. Article 4 removes the automatic right to convert under Class MA, meaning you must apply for full planning permission. This is not a deal-breaker, but it changes the route, the risk profile, and the design approach. Many profitable schemes exist in Article 4 zones, but only when the developer understands the policy context and aligns the proposal with local priorities. You must also review local planning policies that affect residential use.

These may include:

- *Noise and air-quality requirements*
- *Flood-risk constraints*
- *Parking standards*
- *Local space-standard expectations*
- *Heritage or conservation-area restrictions*

Each of these can influence layout, cost, and viability. A planning consultant should review the site before you commit. Their insight protects you from hidden constraints, unrealistic assumptions, and planning risks that could undermine the entire deal.

i. GDV (Gross Development Value) Calculation

GDV Gross Development Value is the financial backbone of every commercial-to-residential conversion. It represents the total market value of all completed units once the project is finished. Every lender, investor, and developer relies on this figure because it determines borrowing capacity, profit margin, and ultimately whether the deal is worth pursuing. If your GDV is wrong, every other calculation collapses. It is the single number that holds the entire appraisal together.

A robust GDV is built on evidence, not optimism. The first step is analyzing comparable sales. You must look at recently sold properties of similar size, type, and finish within a tight radius. Not asking prices actual sold prices. These reveal what the market is genuinely willing to pay. Next, you must understand local demand. Some areas absorb small studios quickly; others favour larger one-bed or two-bed units. Demand shapes value. A beautifully designed unit in a weak market will not achieve a premium, no matter how well it photographs.

Unit size and type also play a major role. Larger units often achieve a lower price per square foot, while smaller, well-designed units can command a premium. Your GDV must reflect the specific mix you intend to build, not a generic average. Location and finish level complete the picture. A high-quality finish in a desirable area can significantly increase value, while a basic finish in a secondary location may cap your ceiling. Buyers and tenants pay for convenience, aesthetics, and lifestyle, not just square footage.

A precise GDV allows you to calculate borrowing capacity, assess profit, and negotiate confidently. An inaccurate GDV, even by a small margin, can turn a promising deal into a financial trap. Getting this number right is not optional, it is the foundation of your entire strategy.

j. Build Cost Estimation & Sensitivity Analysis

Accurate build-cost estimation is one of the most important skills in commercial-to-residential development. A deal that looks profitable on paper can collapse instantly if the construction budget is wrong. Commercial buildings often hide complexities outdated services, structural weaknesses, fire-safety issues that only become visible once work begins. The only protection you have is a disciplined, evidence-based approach to estimating costs and stress-testing your assumptions.

Your build-cost appraisal must include every major component of the conversion. This begins with the strip-out, which can be substantial in older or heavily modified buildings. You must then account for structural work, including steel installation, wall removal, and reinforcement. Plumbing and electrical systems almost always require full replacement, especially when creating multiple units. Fire-safety upgrades are another major cost driver. Residential standards require compartmentation, fire-rated ceilings, protected escape routes, alarms, and sometimes sprinklers. These elements are essential and must be priced realistically.

You must also budget for windows, insulation, partitions, kitchens, bathrooms, flooring, decoration, and all finishing elements. Finally, include professional fees architects, engineers, planning consultants, building-control inspectors and a contingency of 10–15% to protect against unforeseen issues. Once your cost estimate is complete, you must perform a sensitivity analysis. This is how professionals protect themselves from surprises.

Stress-test the deal by asking:

- *What happens if build costs rise by 10%?*
- *What if GDV drops by 5%?*
- *What if the project overruns by 3–6 months?*

If the deal still works under these pressures, you have a robust project. If it collapses, you have identified the risk before committing capital.

Chapter 8: Designing the Residential Layout

Design is where commercial conversion becomes both an art and a science. A building may qualify for Class MA, pass every structural check, and show strong GDV potential but if the internal layout is poor, the project will underperform. Layout is the bridge between compliance and commercial success. It determines how efficiently you use the space, how desirable the units feel, and how well the final product performs in the market.

This chapter gives you a clear, practical framework for designing residential units that meet regulations, maximize value, and appeal to modern tenants and buyers. You will learn how to translate a raw commercial floor plate into a series of functional, attractive homes that comply with building regulations, fire safety, natural-light requirements, and space standards. You will also learn how to design layouts that feel intuitive where circulation flows naturally, rooms are well-proportioned, and every square metre works hard.

Designing a strong layout is not about squeezing in as many units as possible. It is about creating homes that people genuinely want to live in. That means understanding how to position kitchens and bathrooms, how to maximize natural light, how to avoid awkward corners and wasted space, and how to ensure every unit meets the expectations of today's rental and sales markets.

By the end of this chapter, you will be able to look at any commercial building and visualize a layout that is compliant, efficient, and commercially strong. You will understand the principles that turn a blank floor plate into a profitable, high-quality residential scheme and you will be able to design with confidence, clarity, and purpose.

a. Start with the End User in Mind

Before you draw a single line on a floor plan, you must understand exactly who you are designing for. Layout design is not an abstract exercise; it is a response to human behavior, lifestyle patterns, and local demand. A beautifully drawn plan is worthless if it does not meet the needs of the people who will actually live in this space. The most successful developers begin with the end user and work backwards.

Start by asking the fundamental questions:
- *Who will live here*
- *What lifestyle they lead*
- *What price point they are comfortable with*
- *What amenities matter most to them*

These questions shape every design decision from unit size to room placement to the level of finish. A layout designed for young professionals will look very different from one designed for downsizers or students. Understanding your demographic is not optional; it is the foundation of a commercially strong scheme.

Different user groups require different layouts:
- *Young professionals often prefer compact studios, one-bed units, or co-living arrangements. They value open-plan living, modern finishes, and proximity to transport.*
- *Small families need two-bed units with practical storage, functional kitchens, and comfortable living spaces.*
- *Students prioritize affordability, en-suite rooms, and shared social spaces making HMO-style layouts more suitable.*
- *Downsizers look for accessible units, lifts, wider corridors, and layouts that minimize stairs and maximize comfort.*

A successful conversion aligns the building's natural strengths with the needs of the local market. Not every building suit every demographic and that's the point. When you match the right user to the right building, the layout almost designs itself. When you ignore the end user, even the best building will underperform.

b. Minimum Space Standards (The Non-Negotiables)

Minimum space standards are the foundation of good residential design. They ensure that the homes you create are not only compliant, but comfortable, marketable, and financially resilient. While certain Permitted Development routes offer flexibility, the most successful developers treat the Nationally Described Space Standards (NDSS) as their baseline. These standards reflect what modern occupants expect and what lenders, valuers, and buyers increasingly demand.

The NDSS guidelines provide clear minimums:
- *Studio: approx. 37m²*
- *One-bed: approx. 50m²*
- *Two-bed: approx. 61–70m²*
- *HMO rooms: approx. 6.5–10m² depending on configuration*

These numbers are not arbitrary. They are based on decades of research into how people live, move, and use space. When you design below these thresholds, you compromise comfort, functionality, and long-term value. Even if a smaller unit is technically legal under PDR, it may struggle to attract quality tenants, achieve strong valuations, or secure mortgage lending.

Sticking to NDSS improves every aspect of your project:
- *Mortgageability: Lenders prefer units that meet recognized standards.*
- *Market value: Larger, well-designed units command stronger prices.*
- *Tenant demand: People choose homes that feel spacious, not cramped.*
- *Long-term resilience: NDSS-compliant units remain desirable for decades.*

Small units may rent quickly in certain markets, but they rarely deliver sustainable value. They limit your buyer pool, reduce your refinancing options, and expose you to future regulatory tightening. In contrast, NDSS-aligned layouts create homes that appeal to a broad audience and stand the test of time.

Minimum space standards are not a constraint they are a strategic advantage. When you design with them in mind, you create homes that feel natural, functional, and desirable. And in commercial conversions, desirability is what drives both profit and long-term success.

c. Natural Light & Ventilation

Natural light is one of the most important design factors in any commercial-to-residential conversion. It shapes how a home feels, how it functions, and how well it performs in the market. A bright, well-ventilated unit rents faster, sells faster, and commands a premium. A dark, poorly ventilated unit, even if technically compliant will always struggle. This is why natural light, and ventilation must be at the centre of your layout strategy from the very beginning.

The first rule is simple: every habitable room must have a window. Bedrooms, living rooms, and kitchens all require natural light and a practical ventilation route. Windows must be large enough to meet daylight standards, positioned to allow light to penetrate the room, and designed to provide adequate airflow. Internal rooms should be avoided unless absolutely unavoidable they create design compromises, reduce desirability, and often fail to meet modern expectations.

Ventilation is equally important. Mechanical systems can support kitchens and bathrooms, but habitable rooms must have natural ventilation wherever possible. Poor airflow leads to condensation, overheating, and long-term maintenance issues. A well-designed ventilation strategy improves comfort, reduces running costs, and enhances the overall feel of the home.

If the building has deep floor plates, you must think creatively. Options include:

- *Light wells to bring daylight into the centre of the building*
- *Internal courtyards that create shared or private outdoor space*
- *Enlarged windows to increase daylight penetration*
- *Reconfigured layouts that position habitable rooms along the perimeter*

These interventions can transform a challenging building into a bright, attractive residential scheme.

Natural light and ventilation are not aesthetic luxuries they are core components of good design. When you prioritize them, you create homes that feel uplifting, healthy, and valuable. And in commercial conversions, that difference is everything.

d. Fire Safety & Escape Routes

Fire safety is one of the most significant design constraints in any commercial-to-residential conversion. You can create the most elegant, efficient layout on paper, but if it fails fire-safety requirements, the entire scheme becomes unviable. Residential standards are far more demanding than commercial ones, and your design must incorporate these requirements from the very beginning not as an afterthought.

The backbone of fire-safe design is the protected staircase. This is the primary escape route for residents, and it must be enclosed with fire-rated construction that prevents smoke and flames from entering during an emergency. The staircase dictates how units are arranged, how corridors are designed, and how far occupants can travel before reaching safety. Every layout must also include fire-rated partitions between units and between units and common areas. These partitions slow the spread of fire and protect escape routes. The thickness, materials, and rating of these walls must be carefully specified and coordinated with your architect and fire consultant.

Smoke ventilation is another critical factor. Depending on the building's size and configuration, you may need natural ventilation, mechanical smoke extraction, or a combination of both. Poor smoke-ventilation design can invalidate an otherwise compliant layout. You must also respect maximum travel distances the maximum length a resident can travel from their front door to a protected escape route. Exceeding these distances triggers additional fire-safety measures or forces a redesign.

Other essential elements include:

- *Fire doors with appropriate ratings and self-closing mechanisms*
- *Sprinkler systems, which may be required depending on height, layout, or escape distances*

Fire safety is not negotiable. Your architect and fire consultant must work together from day one. A beautiful layout that fails fire-safety standards is worthless, but a layout designed with fire safety at its core becomes both compliant and commercially strong.

e. *Circulation & Flow*

Circulation is one of the most underrated elements of residential design, yet it has an enormous impact on how a home feels. Good design feels effortless if you move through the space naturally, without obstruction or confusion. Poor design, on the other hand, feels cramped, awkward, or disjointed, even if the unit technically meets all space standards. In commercial-to-residential conversions, where floor plates were never intended for domestic use, circulation becomes even more critical.

Start by assessing the fundamentals:

- *Corridor widths must allow comfortable movement and meet accessibility expectations.*
- *Turning circles matter, especially in smaller units or where accessibility is required.*
- *Door swing directions must be logical and avoid clashing with furniture or blocking circulation routes.*
- *Access to bathrooms should be convenient and private, not through kitchens or living rooms.*
- *Privacy between bedrooms and living areas is essential for comfort and market appeal.*

These elements shape the everyday experience of the occupant. A layout that forces residents to squeeze through narrow hallways, navigate awkward door swings, or walk through the kitchen to reach the bathroom will always feel compromised.

Equally important is what you must avoid:

- *Long, dark corridors that waste space and feel oppressive*
- *Narrow hallways that make the unit feel smaller than it is*
- *Bedrooms opening directly into kitchens, which reduce privacy and marketability*
- *Units with no clear flow, where rooms feel disconnected or poorly arranged*

Your goal is to create homes, not boxes. A well-designed layout guides the residents intuitively from one space to the next, balancing openness with privacy and efficiency with comfort. When circulation is done well, the entire unit feels larger, brighter, and more welcoming and that translates directly into stronger demand and higher value.

f. Bin Storage, Cycle Storage & Services

Bin storage, cycle storage, and service routes are some of the most overlooked elements in commercial-to-residential design, yet they are among the first things councils scrutinize. A layout can be elegant, efficient, and beautifully presented, but if it fails to provide adequate waste storage, secure cycle parking, or practical service routes, the scheme may be delayed, reduced in scale, or refused altogether. These components are not optional extras; they are essential infrastructure. Every scheme must include secure cycle storage that meets local standards. Many councils require covered, lockable, and easily accessible cycle spaces, often at ground level. Poorly positioned cycle storage such as spaces hidden behind awkward corridors or located up flights of stairs will not be accepted. Bin storage is equally important. You must provide enough capacity for general waste, recycling, and food waste, depending on local requirements. The store must be accessible for residents and positioned so that waste-collection teams can reach it without obstruction. A bin store that is too small, too far from the street, or located in a way that causes odor or noise issues will trigger objections.

You must also plan for service risers the vertical routes that carry plumbing, electrics, ventilation ducts, and drainage. Without well-positioned risers, your layout becomes inefficient, expensive, or impossible to build. Kitchens and bathrooms should be stacked logically to minimize pipe runs and reduce construction costs. Ventilation routes for kitchens and bathrooms must also be considered early. Mechanical extract systems require ducting, external vents, and fire-safe pathways. Poor planning here can force last-minute redesigns or reduce the number of units you can create.

These elements may not be glamorous, but they are essential. Poor planning can delay Prior Approval, increase build costs, or undermine the entire scheme. Good planning, on the other hand, creates efficient, compliant, and market-ready homes.

g. Designing for Profit: The Developer's Perspective

Designing a residential layout is not just about compliance or aesthetics, it is a commercial exercise. A well-designed layout increases GDV, boosts rental income, improves mortgageability, and enhances market appeal. In commercial-to-residential conversions, where margins can be tight and every square metre carries financial weight, design becomes one of your most powerful profit levers.

The most profitable schemes prioritize the unit types that deliver the strongest demand and the best price per square metre. In most markets, this means focusing on one-bed and two-bed units. These appeal to the widest demographic young professionals, couples, small families, and downsizers and they typically achieve the most balanced blend of value, rentability, and mortgageability. Oversized studios, on the other hand, often underperform. They consume valuable floor area without delivering the uplift in GDV that a well-designed one-bed would achieve.

To maximize profit, your layout must be efficient. Open-plan living helps reduce wasted space, improve natural light, and create a modern feel that appeals to today's tenants and buyers. Stacking plumbing vertically keeps construction costs down and simplifies maintenance. Minimizing corridor space ensures that more of your floor area becomes usable, saleable living space rather than dead circulation.

Symmetry also plays a role. Symmetrical layouts allow repeated unit types, standardized construction, and predictable service routes. This reduces building costs, speeds up construction, and creates a cleaner, more coherent design.

Every square metre matters. A few centimeters saved in a corridor, a smarter bathroom layout, or a more efficient kitchen position can be the difference between squeezing in an extra unit or losing one. And in development, one additional unit can transform the entire appraisal.

Designing for profit is not about cutting corners, it is about designing intelligently. When you combine efficiency, desirability, and market insight, you create homes that perform financially and stand the test of time.

h. Accessibility Requirements

Accessibility is an increasingly important part of residential design, and in many commercial-to-residential conversions it becomes a defining constraint. Depending on the planning route, building regulations, and the building's existing structure, you may be required to meet specific accessibility standards, most commonly M4(1), which sets out the baseline requirements for accessible and adaptable homes. Meeting accessibility standards can influence several aspects of your layout. You may need wider doorways, step-free entrances, and circulation spaces that allow comfortable movement throughout the unit. In multi-storey buildings, lift access may be required, especially if you are creating multiple units above ground level. These requirements must be considered early, as retrofitting accessibility into a completed design is costly and often impractical.

Even when accessibility is not strictly required under PDR, incorporating accessible features increases the long-term value and resilience of your scheme. The population is ageing, mobility needs are rising, and lenders increasingly favor developments that meet modern standards. Accessible units appeal to a broader market, rent more easily, and remain compliant as regulations evolve. Accessibility is not just a regulatory box to tick it is a strategic design choice. When you build with inclusivity in mind, your future-proof your development and creates homes that serve a wider community.

i. Working with an Architect

Choosing the right architect is one of the most important decisions you will make in a commercial-to-residential conversion. Not all architects are created equal, and not all have the skill set required to turn a commercial floor plate into efficient, compliant, desirable homes. A commercial architect who specializes in offices or retail units is rarely suitable. You need someone who understands how people live, not just how they work.

Your architect must have a strong grasp of Permitted Development Rights (PDR), especially Class MA. Residential conversions under PDR come with unique constraints around natural light, fire safety, space standards, and noise mitigation. An architect who does not understand these rules will design layouts that look attractive but fail at

Prior Approval. They must also understand residential design principles, how to create intuitive circulation, how to position kitchens and bathrooms efficiently, how to maximize natural light, and how to design units that feel modern and comfortable. Residential design is a different discipline from commercial design, and it requires a different mindset.

Fire safety is another essential area. Your architect must be able to work seamlessly with a fire consultant to ensure protected staircases, fire-rated partitions, escape distances, and smoke-ventilation strategies are integrated from day one. A layout that fails fire safety is not a layout it is a sketch.

Finally, your architect must understand cost-efficient design. Beautiful drawings are meaningless if they cannot be built affordably. Efficient plumbing stacks, logical riser placement, repeated unit types, and minimal wasted space all contribute to a commercially strong scheme.

The right architect elevates your project. The wrong one costs you time, money, and opportunity.

Part 4: Finance, Legals & Execution

Part 4 is where your commercial-to-residential journey becomes real. Up to this point, you've learned how to analyze buildings, design layouts, and understand the technical constraints that shape a viable scheme. But none of that matters unless you can fund the project, structure the legal agreements correctly, manage the building efficiently, and protect yourself from risk. This part of the book takes you behind the scenes of how professional developers operate the systems, documents, financial structures, and decision-making frameworks that turn a good idea into a completed, profitable development.

Many beginners believe development is about finding a building and hiring a builder. Professionals know it is far more strategic. The success or failure of a project is often determined long before construction begins in the funding structure, the legal paperwork, the consultant team, and the risk-management approach. This part of the book gives you the tools to operate at that level.

Chapter 9: Funding the Conversion

Here you'll learn how to finance a commercial conversion using a combination of bridging finance, development loans, private investors, and your own capital. You'll understand how lenders assess risk, how to present your deal professionally, and how to structure funding so that cash flow remains stable throughout the project. You'll also learn how GDV, build cost, and contingency influence borrowing capacity and how to avoid the common funding mistakes that derail new developers.

Chapter 10: Legal Agreements & Compliance Documents

This chapter demystifies the legal side of development. You'll learn the essential agreements you must have in place from purchase contracts and warranties to party-wall notices, building-control approvals, and consultant appointments. You'll also understand the compliance documents required for planning, construction, and eventual sale or refinance. This is where you learn to protect yourself legally and ensure your project is built on solid foundations.

Chapter 11: Project Management & Value Engineering
A development is only as strong as its execution. This chapter shows you how to manage contractors, control costs, sequence work and keep the project moving. You'll learn how to value-engineer intelligently reduce costs without reducing quality and how to avoid the delays, disputes, and inefficiencies that destroy profit. Whether you manage the project yourself or hire a professional, this chapter gives you the framework to stay in control.

Chapter 12: Risk Management
Every development carries risk. Professionals don't avoid risks, they identify it early, price it correctly, and put systems in place to manage it. This chapter teaches you how to anticipate structural risks, planning risks, funding risks, contractor risks, and market risks. You'll learn how to build contingencies, how to stress-test your appraisal, and how to make decisions that protect your downside while preserving your upside.

Chapter 13: Build to Rent vs Build to Sell
Finally, you'll explore the two main exit strategies: selling the units or holding them as long-term rentals. Each path has different financial implications, tax considerations, and design priorities. This chapter helps you choose the right strategy for your goals, your market, and your long-term wealth plan.

Chapter 14: Making the Right Offers Consistently
This chapter brings together everything you've learned so far and applies it to one of the most decisive moments in development: the offer. You'll learn how professional developers calculate offers using

GDV, conservative cost planning, and required profit margins. You'll understand how to stress-test deals, price in risk, and avoid the emotional decision-making that leads to overpaying. You'll also discover how to present offers with clarity and confidence, how to build trust with agents and sellers, and how to make offers consistently so you secure more opportunities. This chapter gives you the discipline and structure needed to act like a professional not a hopeful buyer.

Chapter 9: Funding the Conversion

9.1 Bridging Finance for Acquisition

Bridging finance is the engine that powers most commercial-to-residential conversions. Traditional mortgages are too slow, too restrictive, and unsuitable for buildings that require change of use or significant refurbishment. Bridging loans, on the other hand, are designed for speed, flexibility, and short-term acquisition making them the primary tool for securing commercial buildings before converting them into residential units.

A bridging loan is a short-term, interest-only facility used to purchase a property quickly, usually for 6–18 months. The lender advances funds based on the building's current value and the strength of your proposed exit strategy. Because commercial conversions often involve planning, construction, and refinancing, bridging lenders focus heavily on the viability of the project rather than just the asset itself.

Lenders assess risk using several key factors:

- *Purchase price vs current value*
- *Your experience and track record*
- *The strength of the GDV and appraisal*
- *Planning route (Class MA vs full planning)*
- *Build cost estimates and contingency*
- *Exit strategy (refinance or sale)*

Typical terms include 65–75% loan-to-value on day one, rolled-up interest, lender fees, and a requirement for a clear, realistic plan. Rates are higher than traditional mortgages, but the speed and flexibility they offer make them indispensable for developers. To make your deal attractive to a bridging provider, you must present a clear, evidence-based proposal. This includes a robust GDV, a realistic build budget, a credible timeline, and a defined exit. Lenders want confidence that you understand the project, the risks, and the numbers. When you demonstrate this, funding becomes far easier to secure even as a newer developer.

Bridging finance is not just a loan; it is a strategic tool. Used correctly, it allows you to move fast, secure opportunities others miss, and unlock the value hidden inside commercial buildings.

9.2 Development Finance for the Build

Once you've acquired the building using bridging finance, the next stage is funding the construction itself. This is where development finance comes in a specialist loan designed to cover the cost of the build, professional fees, and sometimes even part of the interest. Development finance is the engine that turns a raw commercial shell into completed residential units.

Unlike a bridging loan, development finance is released in staged drawdowns. You don't receive the full amount upfront. Instead, funds are released as the project progresses. Each drawdown is triggered by a monitoring surveyor (often called an MS), appointed by the lender. Their job is to visit the site, confirm that the completed works match the cost plan, and ensure the project is on track. Only then will the lender release the next tranche of funds. This means your cost plan must be detailed, realistic, and professionally prepared. Lenders want to see a clear breakdown of labor, materials, preliminaries, professional fees, and contingency. If your numbers are vague or overly optimistic, funding delays are almost guaranteed.

Development finance typically charges interest monthly, either serviced or rolled up. Some lenders offer interest-retention, where part of the loan is set aside to cover interest during the build. This protects your cash flow but reduces the amount available for construction.

The most common pitfalls include:

- *Underestimating build costs*
- *Failing to provide updated QS reports*
- *Delays in contractor mobilization*
- *Poor communication with the monitoring surveyor*

• *Drawdown requests submitted without proper evidence*
Any of these can stall funding and disrupt the entire project.
Development finance is not just money it is a controlled, monitored system. When you understand how it works and manage it proactively, it becomes a powerful tool that keeps your project funded, structured, and moving forward.

9.3 GDV-Based Lending Explained

GDV-based lending is one of the most powerful financial tools available to developers. Instead of lending purely against the property's current value, some lenders assess the deal based on its Gross Development Value the total value of the completed units once the conversion is finished. This approach allows you to borrow more, move faster, and take on projects that would be impossible using traditional value-based lending alone. To understand GDV lending, you must understand how lenders calculate GDV.

They look at:

• *Comparable sales within a tight radius*
• *Unit mix and sizes in your proposed layout*
• *Local demand and absorption rates*
• *Finish level and specification*
• *Market conditions at completion*

Lenders do not rely on your optimism. They rely on evidence. If your GDV is inflated, vague, or unsupported, the lender will reduce it and your borrowing capacity will fall with it.

GDV lending is powerful because it allows lenders to fund a higher percentage of the project. Instead of lending 65–75% of the current value, they may lend up to 65% of the GDV, plus a portion of the build costs. This means you can acquire and convert buildings with far less upfront capital, provided the numbers stack and the exit is strong.

To withstand lender scrutiny, your GDV must be:

• *Evidence-based, using real sold comparables*
• *Specific, broken down by unit type and size*
• *Conservative, not based on best-case scenarios*

• *Aligned with your layout, not generic averages*
• *Supported by an independent valuation, where required*

A lender wants to see that your GDV is realistic, your build costs are credible, and your exit strategy is achievable. When your numbers are clear, defensible, and professionally presented, GDV-based lending becomes a powerful accelerator enabling you to scale faster and take on more ambitious conversions.

9.4 Private Investors and Joint Ventures

Private investors are one of the most powerful funding sources available to a developer not because they replace lenders, but because they allow you to scale faster, reduce your personal capital input, and unlock deals that would otherwise be out of reach. But raising private capital must be done ethically, transparently, and professionally. Investors are not just providing money; they are placing trust in your ability to deliver.

Understanding investor psychology is essential. Most private investors are not looking for maximum return they are looking for security, clarity, and competence.

They want to know:

• *Their capital is protected*
• *The project is well-researched*
• *You have a clear plan and exit*
• *You communicate consistently*
• *You can handle challenges professionally*

When you demonstrate these qualities, raising capital becomes far easier. Joint ventures (JVs) are a more formal structure where two or more parties share risk, reward, and responsibility. A JV must be built on aligned expectations.

This means agreeing upfront on:

•*Roles and responsibilities*
• *Profit splits*
• *Decision-making authority*
• *Exit strategy*

• *What happens if things go wrong*

A well-drafted JV agreement protects both parties. It should be prepared by a solicitor experienced in development partnerships, not downloaded from the internet or copied from another deal. The agreement must cover capital contributions, dispute resolution, timelines, reporting requirements, and what happens if additional funds are needed.

The key to long-term funding relationships is professionalism. Provide regular updates. Share progress photos. Be honest about challenges. Deliver projects on time and on budget. When investors feel informed and respected, they reinvest and they introduce you to others.

Private capital is not about persuasion. It is about alignment, transparency, and trust. When you operate with integrity and competence, investors become long-term partners who help you scale your development business far beyond what your own capital could achieve.

9.5 Presenting Deals Professionally to Lenders and Investors

How you present a deal is just as important as the deal itself. Lenders and investors are not simply assessing the building they are assessing as you. Your clarity, professionalism, and ability to communicate the numbers determine whether people trust you with their capital. A strong deal, poorly presented, will struggle. A good deal, presented with authority, will attract funding.

A professional deal pack begins with a clear, evidence-based appraisal. This includes your purchase price, build cost, contingency, professional fees, finance costs, and projected GDV. Every number must be justified. Guesswork destroys credibility. Lenders and investors want to see that you understand the financial mechanics of the project and have stress-tested your assumptions. Next, you must include comparables real sold data, not asking prices. Break them down by unit type, size, and finish level. Show how your proposed units align with the local market. When your comparables are tight, relevant, and well-explained, your GDV becomes far more defensible.

A strong deal pack also includes a risk assessment. Professionals don't pretend risks don't exist, they identify them early and explain how they will be managed. Highlight planning risks, build risks, funding risks, and market risks, along with your mitigation strategies. This demonstrates maturity and competence. Your exit strategy must be clear and realistic. Whether you plan to refinance, sell, or hold, explain the timeline, the lender requirements, and the financial logic behind your decision. Investors want to know how and when they get their money back.

Finally, communicate with authority. Use clean layouts, simple language, and structured logic. Avoid jargon. Present yourself as someone who understands the project, the numbers, and the responsibilities involved. When you package a deal professionally, you don't just present an opportunity you present yourself as a developer worth backing.

Chapter 10: Legal Agreements & Compliance Documents

10.1 Confidentiality Agreements or Non-Disclosure Agreements (NDAs) (NDAs)

Confidentiality Agreements commonly known as NDAs play a subtle but important role in professional property development. While not required for every deal, they are essential whenever sensitive information is being shared between parties. In commercial-to-residential conversions, NDAs help protect intellectual property, financial data, investor details, and off-market opportunities. They create a safe environment for open discussion and demonstrate that you operate with professionalism and integrity.

An NDA is a simple legal document that prevents one party from sharing or misusing information provided by another.

In property deals, this might include:

- *Off-market opportunities shared by agents or sources*
- *Vendor circumstances that must remain private*
- *Your appraisal, layout concepts, or planning strategy*
- *Investor details, funding structures, or JV terms*
- *Commercially sensitive negotiations*

Using an Non-Disclosure Agreements (NDAs) A signal that you take confidentiality seriously. Agents and deal sources are far more willing to share high-quality opportunities when they know their information won't be circulated or used without permission. Investors also appreciate NDAs because they protect their identity, capital position, and personal circumstances.

Non-Disclosure Agreements (NDAs) are particularly useful when exploring joint ventures. Before you share your appraisal, comparables, build strategy, or financial model, an NDA ensures that the other party cannot take your work and pursue the deal independently. It protects your time, your intellectual property, and your commercial advantage. However, Non-Disclosure Agreements (NDAs) are not a substitute for trust they are a foundation for it. They show that you operate professionally, respect confidentiality, and understand the importance of safeguarding sensitive information. In an industry built on relationships, this matters. A well-drafted Non-Disclosure Agreements (NDAs) is simple, clear, and fair. It protects both parties and sets the tone for a transparent, respectful working relationship. When used correctly, NDAs strengthen partnerships, unlock better opportunities, and elevate your reputation as a serious developer.

10.2 Finder's Fee Agreements

Finder's fees are a normal and legitimate part of the property industry. Deal sources, agents, and introducers often bring opportunities you would never have found on your own and they deserve to be compensated when they add genuine value. But finder's fees must be handled professionally, transparently, and in full compliance with UK property-sourcing regulations. A poorly drafted agreement can lead to disputes, regulatory breaches, or even the loss of a deal. A finder's fee agreement sets out the terms under which a sourcer introduces a property opportunity to you.

At minimum, it should clearly define:

- *The property being introduced*
- *The fee amount and when it becomes payable*
- *What constitutes a "successful introduction"*
- *Whether the fee is refundable*
- *The sourcer's responsibilities*
- *Your responsibilities*
- *Compliance obligations (AML, due diligence, redress schemes)*

A compliant agreement protects both parties. For the sourcer, it ensures they are paid fairly for their work. For the developer, it ensures the sourcer is operating legally, has the right permissions, and is not misrepresenting the deal. In the UK, deal sourcers must be registered with a redress scheme, hold PI insurance, and comply with anti-money-laundering regulations. Your agreement should confirm these points explicitly.

One of the biggest causes of dispute is ambiguity, especially around when the fee becomes due. Some sourcers expect payment on offer acceptance, others on exchange, and others on completion. Your agreement must state this clearly. It should also specify what happens if the deal collapses through no fault of the sourcer. Another common issue is double-selling, where a sourcer introduces the same deal to multiple investors. A strong agreement prevents this by defining exclusivity and requiring the sourcer to confirm they have authority to introduce the property.

A well-structured finder's fee agreement builds trust, reduces risk, and ensures that both parties operate professionally. When handled correctly, it becomes a smooth, predictable part of your acquisition process not a source of conflict.

10.3 Terms of Business with Agents and Consultants

Professional developers formalize every key relationship not because they expect conflict, but because clarity prevents it. When working with architects, planners, surveyors, commercial agents, and other consultants, a clear Terms of Business agreement sets expectations, defines responsibilities, and ensures everyone understands the scope of work from day one. Without this structure, misunderstandings become inevitable, timelines slip, and costs escalate.

A strong Terms of Business document begins with a clear scope of work. This outlines exactly what the consultant will deliver, by when, and in what format. For an architect, this might include concept layouts, planning drawings, building-regulation packages, and coordination with structural and fire consultants. For a planner, it may include planning statements, policy reviews, and managing the Prior Approval process. For a surveyor, it could cover cost plans, valuations, and monitoring duties. Ambiguity is the enemy, the more specific the scope, the smoother the project.

Next, the agreement must define fees and payment terms. This includes fixed fees, hourly rates, staged payments, and any additional charges for variations or extra work. Many disputes arise because a consultant believes a task is outside scope, while the developer assumes it is included. Clear fee structures eliminate this friction.

Responsibilities must also be explicit. Who submits the planning application? Who liaises with building control? Who coordinates drawings? Who updates the cost plan? When responsibilities overlap, delays and duplication occur. Professional standards matter too. Your agreement should reference the consultant's regulatory body, insurance requirements, and expected level of service. This protects you if performance falls below acceptable standards.

Finally, include terms for communication, timelines, confidentiality, and dispute resolution. These ensure that if challenges arise and they always do there is a clear process for resolving them. Formal Terms of Business don't slow a project down. They accelerate it by creating alignment, accountability, and a shared understanding of what success looks like.

10.4 Reservation Agreements

A reservation agreement is one of the simplest yet most effective tools for securing a property deal. In a market where speed, clarity, and commitment matter, a reservation agreement creates certainty between buyer and seller during the early stages of a transaction. It prevents misunderstandings, reduces the risk of gas pumping, and sets out the expectations that will govern the deal until exchange of contracts.

At its core, a reservation agreement temporarily removes the property from the open market in exchange for a small fee or written commitment. This gives you the breathing space to carry out due diligence, instruct solicitors, finalize funding, and complete surveys without the fear of another buyer stepping in. For the seller, it provides reassurance that you are serious, credible, and financially committed to progressing the purchase.

A strong reservation agreement should clearly define:

- *The agreed purchase price*
- *The reservation period (typically 14–28 days)*
- *Whether a reservation fee is payable*
- *What happens if either party withdraws*
- *What information must be provided during the reservation period*
- *Any conditions, such as funding approval or survey results*

The agreement should also specify that the seller will not negotiate with other buyers during the reservation period. This prevents galumphing, a common issue in competitive markets where sellers are tempted by higher offers after accepting yours. For developers, reservation agreements are especially valuable when dealing with commercial agents or motivated vendors. They demonstrate professionalism, reduce uncertainty, and create a structured pathway toward exchange. They also help maintain momentum, as both parties understand the timeline and their responsibilities. A well-drafted reservation agreement does not replace the formal contract it precedes it. But it sets the tone for a transparent, committed transaction and significantly increases the likelihood of a smooth, timely exchange.

10.5 Assignment Agreements

Assignment agreements allow one party to transfer their rights or interest in a property contract to another party. In development, assignments are used strategically to pass on a deal, transfer contractual rights, or restructure who ultimately completes the purchase. When handled correctly, assignments can unlock opportunities and create flexibility. When handled poorly, they create legal risk, disputes, and reputational damage.

At its core, an assignment is the transfer of a contractual right from one party (the assignor) to another (the assignee). In property, this typically involves assigning the benefit of a purchase contract, an option agreement, or an exclusivity arrangement. Assignments are common when a developer secures a deal but chooses not to complete it themselves often because they want to package and sell the opportunity to another investor.

A legally sound assignment agreement must clearly define:

- *The contract or rights being assigned*
- *The parties involved*
- *The assignment fee (if applicable)*
- *When the fee becomes payable*
- *Any conditions or restrictions*
- *Liabilities and responsibilities after assignment*

It is essential to understand that you can only assign rights you legally hold. If your original contract prohibits assignment or requires the seller's consent, you must comply. Assigning a contract without permission can invalidate the deal and expose you to legal action.

Ethical structuring is equally important. Assignments should never be used to mislead sellers, inflate prices unfairly, or hide your intentions. Transparency protects your reputation and ensures long-term relationships with agents, vendors, and investors.

Assignments can be powerful when used correctly. They allow you to monetize opportunities, collaborate with other developers, and structure deals creatively. But they must be drafted by a solicitor, executed with clarity, and grounded in ethical practice. When handled professionally, assignment agreements become a flexible tool in your development toolkit enabling you to move strategically and profitably in a competitive market.

10.6 Heads of Terms

Heads of Terms (HoTs) are one of the most important documents in any property transaction. They are not legally binding, but they act as the blueprint for the formal contract your solicitors will later draft. When done well, they streamline negotiations, reduce misunderstandings, and prevent costly delays. When done poorly or skipped entirely the transaction becomes vulnerable to confusion, disputes, and shifting expectations.

The purpose of Heads of Terms is simple: to set out the key commercial points of the deal in clear, agreed language before solicitors begin their work. This ensures that both parties understand the structure, the price, the responsibilities, and the timeline. Solicitors rely on HoTs to draft the contract efficiently. Without them, they are forced to guess intentions, seek clarification, and renegotiate points that should have been settled earlier.

A strong set of Heads of Terms should include:

- *The agreed purchase price*
- *The parties involved*
- *The property details*
- *Deposit amount and payment terms*
- *Timescales for exchange and completion*
- *Any conditions (planning, funding, surveys, vacant possession)*
- *Responsibility for legal fees*
- *Access rights for surveys and due diligence*
- *Any special arrangements (assignability, overage, lease terms, warranties)*

HoTs also help manage expectations. If the seller expects a quick exchange but you require time for funding approval or structural surveys, this must be stated upfront. If you need early access for architects or contractors, it should be included. Clarity now prevents conflict later.

For developers, Heads of Terms are essential because they create momentum. Once both parties sign, the deal becomes structured, predictable, and far less likely to drift. Agents also prefer HoTs because they demonstrate commitment and reduce the risk of the transaction collapsing.

In short, Heads of Terms turn verbal agreements into a clear roadmap. They protect relationships, guide solicitors, and ensure the deal progresses smoothly from negotiation to exchange.

10.7 Exclusivity Agreements

Exclusivity agreements are one of the most effective tools for protecting your position in a competitive property market. When you identify a strong commercial-to-residential opportunity, the last thing you want is another buyer stepping in with a higher offer or faster timeline. An exclusivity agreement prevents this by giving you a legally recognized period during which the seller cannot negotiate with anyone else. It creates certainty, reduces risk, and gives you the time you need to complete due diligence properly.

At its core, an exclusivity agreement is a simple contract: in exchange for a commitment, often a small fee or a clear demonstration of readiness the seller agrees not to entertain other offers for a defined period. This period is typically 14–28 days but can be longer for complex commercial buildings requiring structural surveys, planning advice, or lender approval.

A strong exclusivity agreement should clearly set out:

- *The exclusivity period and when it begins*
- *The seller's obligation not to negotiate with other parties*
- *Your obligations, such as progressing surveys or funding*
- *Any exclusivity fee and whether it is refundable*
- *Access rights for due diligence*
- *Consequences if either party breaches the agreement*

For developers, exclusivity is especially valuable when dealing with motivated vendors, probate sales, off-market opportunities, or agents who want reassurance that you are committed. It protects the time and money you invest in appraisals, architect visits, QS reports, and lender discussions.

Exclusivity also strengthens your negotiating position. When a seller commits to you formally, the emotional and commercial momentum shifts. They become invested in completing the deal with you, not shopping around for alternatives. While an exclusivity agreement does not replace the formal contract, it creates a secure window in which you can work confidently, without fear of competition or last-minute surprises. In a fast-moving market, that certainty is invaluable.

10.8 Anti-Money Laundering (AML) Requirements

Anti-Money Laundering (AML) regulations are a fundamental part of the UK property industry. Whether you are a developer, investor, sourcer, or agent, you operate within a regulated environment designed to prevent criminal funds from entering the property market. Compliance is not optional it is a legal obligation. Understanding AML requirements protects your business, strengthens your credibility, and ensures your transactions withstand scrutiny from lenders, solicitors, and regulators.

At the core of AML compliance are identity checks. Before entering into a financial relationship, you must verify the identity of investors, JV partners, and in some cases vendors. This typically involves collecting photo ID, proof of address, and verifying authenticity through approved systems. These checks demonstrate that you know who you are dealing with and that their involvement is legitimate.

Equally important is source of funds (SOF) and source of wealth (SOW) verification. Investors must show where their money comes from savings, business profits, property sales, inheritance, or other legitimate sources. As a developer, you must review this documentation and ensure it is consistent, reasonable, and traceable. Lenders and solicitors will also request this information, so gathering it early prevents delays.

Developers also have reporting duties. If you encounter suspicious behavior inconsistent financial information, reluctance to provide documentation, or attempts to obscure ownership you may be legally required to file a Suspicious Activity Report (SAR). Failing to report when required can lead to serious penalties.

To stay compliant, you should:

- *Use approved AML verification tools*
- *Keep clear records of checks and documents*
- *Request Statement of Facts (SOF)/ Statement of Work (SOW) early in the relationship*
- *Work only with investors who cooperate transparently*
- *Ensure deal sourcers you work with are Anti-Money Laundry (AML)registered*

Anti-Money Laundry (AML) compliance is not just a regulatory box to tick. It is a marker of professionalism. When you handle AML properly, you protect your business, reassure your partners, and build a reputation as a trustworthy, credible developer.

10.9 Compliance Packs (Energy Performance Certificate (EPC), Asbestos, Structural, Fire Reports)

A professional developer never relies on assumptions. Before committing to a commercial-to-residential conversion, you must build a complete compliance pack a set of essential reports that confirm the building is safe, viable, and financeable. Lenders, valuers, and solicitors all rely on these documents to assess risk. Without them, funding stalls, valuations fall, and unexpected costs emerge mid-project. A strong compliance pack protects you from surprises and demonstrates that you operate with diligence and professionalism.

The first component is the Energy Performance Certificate (EPC). Commercial buildings often have poor energy ratings, and lenders want assurance that your conversion will meet residential standards. A low EPC may influence valuation, trigger additional upgrade costs, or affect your exit strategy. Understanding this early allows you to budget correctly and avoid last-minute compliance issues.

Next is the asbestos survey. Many commercial buildings especially older offices, warehouses, and industrial units contain asbestos. A full refurbishment or demolition survey identifies where asbestos is located and how it must be removed. Asbestos removal can be expensive, and lenders will not release funds without clarity on the risk and cost implications.

A structural report is equally important. It assesses the integrity of the building, identifies defects, and confirms whether the structure can support your proposed layouts. Structural issues can dramatically affect valuation and may require significant remedial works. Lenders rely heavily on this report to determine whether the building is a safe and viable asset.

Finally, a fire risk assessment or fire strategy report is essential for conversions. It outlines escape routes, compartmentation, fire-rated materials, and compliance with building regulations. Fire safety failures are one of the biggest reasons lenders decline funding.

Together, these documents form the backbone of your due diligence. A complete compliance pack increases lender confidence, strengthens your valuation, and ensures your project begins on solid, predictable ground.

10.10 Disclaimers and Investor Protection Language

When raising capital, how you communicate is just as important as the deal itself. Professional developers use clear, responsible, and legally compliant language to protect both themselves and their investors. Disclaimers are not about being defensive, they are about setting honest expectations, reducing misunderstandings, and demonstrating that you operate with integrity. Investors respect transparency, and regulators require it.

The first principle is risk disclosure. Every investment carries risk, and you must state this clearly. This includes market risk, planning risk, construction risk, funding risk, and exit risk. Your language should make it clear that returns are not guaranteed, timelines may change, and capital is at risk. Responsible developers never promise fixed returns unless they are structured legally and backed by appropriate agreements.

Next is clarity of role. You must explain whether you are acting as a developer, introducer, or JV partner. If you are not regulated to give financial advice, you must state this explicitly. This protects you from unintentionally crossing into regulated activity and ensures investors understand that they must make their own informed decisions.

Your communication should also include transparency statements outlining how investor funds will be used, how decisions are made, and how updates will be provided. Investors want to know that their capital is handled responsibly, with clear reporting and proper oversight. A strong disclaimer also clarifies exit expectations. Explain that refinancing depends on lender criteria, valuations, and market conditions. Explain that sales depend on demand, pricing, and absorption rates. This prevents unrealistic assumptions and reinforces your professionalism.

Finally, disclaimers protect you legally. They show that you have communicated risks, avoided guarantees, and encouraged investors to seek independent advice. When combined with clear documentation and ethical behavior, they form the foundation of long-term,

Chapter 11: Project Management & Value Engineering

11.1 Selecting and Managing Contractors

Selecting the right contractor is one of the most important decisions in any commercial-to-residential conversion. A strong contractor will protect your budget, maintain momentum, and deliver a high-quality finish. The wrong contractor will drain your time, inflate your costs, and jeopardize your entire project. Professional developers treat contractor selection as a rigorous vetting process not a casual hire.

The first step is capability assessment. Commercial conversions require contractors who understand structural alterations, fire-rated construction, acoustic requirements, and the technical demands of residential compliance. A contractor who only builds extensions or refurbishes houses is rarely suitable. You need a team with proven experience in multi-unit conversions, commercial buildings, or similar scale projects.

Next is due diligence. This includes checking references, reviewing previous projects, verifying insurance, confirming accreditations, and assessing financial stability. A contractor who cannot provide evidence of past performance or who avoids transparency is a risk you cannot afford. Once selected, the relationship must be formalized through a clear contract structure.

This should include:

- *A detailed scope of works*
- *A fixed or clearly defined pricing model*
- *A payment schedule tied to milestones*
- *Program timelines*
- *Variation procedures*
- *Insurance and warranty requirements*

Ambiguity is the enemy. A vague contract invites disputes, delays, and cost overruns.

Effective project management depends on communication discipline. Weekly site meetings, written progress updates, and clear decision pathways keep the project aligned. You must remain in control not by micromanaging, but by setting expectations, monitoring progress, and addressing issues early.

Finally, maintain commercial authority. Contractors respect developers who are organized, decisive, and consistent. When you understand your drawings, your cost plan, and your program, you lead from a position of strength. Selecting and managing contractors is not just about hiring a builder. It is about building a professional partnership that delivers your vision on time, on budget, and to the standard your end buyers or tenants expect.

11.2 Programme, Milestones, and Critical Path

A commercial-to-residential conversion succeeds or fails on its program. Time is money in development every delay increases finance costs, disrupts cash flow, and erodes profit. A realistic, well-structured programme is not just a scheduling tool; it is a risk-management system that keeps the project aligned, predictable, and under control. A strong programme begins with a logical sequence of works. This includes strip-out, structural alterations, first fix, inspections, second fix, testing, and final finishes. Each stage must be mapped with realistic durations, dependencies, and allowances for lead times. Over-optimistic programs are one of the biggest causes of cost overruns.

The heart of the programme is the critical path the chain of tasks that directly determines the project's completion date. If any task on the critical path is delayed, the entire project is delayed. In commercial conversions, typical critical path items include structural works, fire-rated partitions, M&E installation, and key inspections. Identifying these early allows you to focus your attention where it matters most. Milestones provide structure and accountability.

These include:
- *Completion of strip-out*
- *Structural sign-off*
- *First-fix completion*
- *Building control inspections*
- *Second-fix completion*
- *Practical completion*

Milestones should be tied to contractor payments, lender drawdowns, and reporting cycles. This ensures that progress is measurable and that everyone understands what must be achieved before funds are released.
Dependencies must also be managed carefully. For example, M&E cannot begin until structural works are complete; plastering cannot begin until first fix is signed off; and final finishes cannot begin until the building is watertight. Ignoring dependencies leads to rework, disputes, and wasted labor
A disciplined programme is reviewed weekly, updated regularly, and communicated clearly. When you manage the programme proactively not reactively you maintain control, protect your budget, and deliver your conversion on time.

11.3 Cost Control and Change Management

Cost control is one of the defining skills of a successful developer. Even a well-designed commercial-to-residential conversion can lose profitability if costs drift, variations multiply, or decisions are made reactively. Professional developers treat cost control as continuous discipline not a one-off task. It begins before construction starts and continues until the final invoice is paid.
The foundation of cost control is a detailed, realistic cost plan. This includes materials, labor, preliminaries, professional fees, contingencies, and finance costs. Once the project begins, this cost plan becomes your baseline. Every decision, variation, and invoice is measured against it. Without a baseline, you cannot track deviations or identify early warning signs. During construction, the key is active monitoring. This means reviewing contractor valuations, checking invoices against agreed milestones, and verifying that completed work

matches what is being billed. Developers who simply "trust the process" often discover overspends too late. Discipline protects your margin.
Variations are the biggest threat to budget integrity. Some variations are unavoidable structural discoveries, regulatory requirements, or unforeseen conditions. Others arise from design changes, specification upgrades, or unclear drawings.

To manage variations effectively, you must:
- *Require all variations to be priced before work begins*
- *Approve variations in writing*
- *Challenge unnecessary or inflated costs*
- *Track cumulative variation totals against contingency*

Fair negotiation is essential. You want contractors to be profitable and motivated, but you must also protect your project. A variation should reflect genuine additional work not inefficiency or poor planning.
Finally, maintain financial discipline. Avoid scope creep. Stick to your specification. Resist impulsive upgrades. Every change has a cost, and every cost affects your return. Cost control is not about being adversarial. It is about being organized, informed, and commercially aware. When you manage costs proactively, you protect your profit, maintain lender confidence, and deliver a financially successful conversion.

11.4 Value Engineering Without Cutting Safety or Quality

Value engineering is not about cheapening a project, it is about maximizing efficiency without compromising safety, compliance, or long-term durability. In commercial-to-residential conversions, intelligent value engineering can protect your margin, accelerate delivery, and improve the final product. Poor value engineering, on the other hand, leads to defects, regulatory failures, and expensive remedial work. The goal is to reduce cost strategically, not recklessly.

The first step is design efficiency. Many savings come from simplifying layouts, reducing unnecessary structural alterations, and standardizing unit types. Every wall moved, beam installed, or bespoke detail added increases cost. A clean, logical design reduces labor, materials, and risk. Early collaboration with your architect, structural engineer, and contractor ensures the design is efficient before construction begins. Material choices also offer significant opportunities.

Value engineering does not mean choosing the cheapest materials, it means selecting materials that deliver the required performance at the best value. For example, choosing durable mid-range finishes instead of premium brands, or selecting compliant fire-rated systems that are easier to install, can reduce cost without affecting quality. Sequencing is another powerful lever. Poor sequencing leads to rework, delays, and wasted labor. Efficient sequencing such as grouping similar tasks, coordinating trades, and ensuring materials arrive just in time reduces downtime and improves productivity. This is where a strong programme and disciplined site management pay dividends.

Specification adjustments can also deliver savings. This might include simplifying lighting layouts, use standardized bathroom packs, or selecting cost-effective heating solutions that still meet EPC and building-regulation requirements. The key is to maintain compliance and performance while avoiding unnecessary upgrades. True value engineering protects the building's safety, integrity, and long-term durability. It requires knowledge, discipline, and collaboration, not shortcuts. When done correctly, it strengthens your project, protects your profit, and delivers a high-quality product your buyers or tenants will trust.

11.5 Handling Unforeseen Issues (Asbestos, HVAC, Structural Surprises)

No matter how thorough your due diligence, commercial-to-residential conversions will always present unforeseen issues. Older buildings hide surprises behind walls, above ceilings, and beneath floors. The developers who succeed are not the ones who avoid problems they are the ones who respond calmly, decisively, and professionally when challenges arise. Unforeseen issues are not project-killers; they are

management tests.
One of the most common surprises is asbestos. Even with a refurbishment survey, asbestos can be discovered during strip-out in unexpected locations. When this happens, the key is to stop work immediately, bring in a licensed contractor, and obtain a revised removal plan. Asbestos issues affect cost, programme, and lender confidence but when handled transparently and professionally, they remain manageable. Structural surprises are another frequent challenge. Hidden steelwork, unsupported walls, rotten timbers, or unexpected load paths can emerge once the building is opened up. The solution is rapid coordination between your structural engineer and contractor. You must obtain revised calculations, updated drawings, and a clear costed plan before proceeding. Guesswork is dangerous; clarity protects both safety and budget.

HVAC and ventilation issues also arise often in commercial conversions. Existing ductwork may be unusable, ceiling voids may be too shallow, or airflow requirements may exceed initial assumptions. Early engagement with your M&E engineer is essential. Sometimes the solution is redesign; sometimes it is upgrading plant; sometimes it is re-routing services. The key is to address the issue before plasterboard goes up.

Drainage surprises collapsed pipes, insufficient capacity, or unknown connections can also disrupt progress. CCTV surveys and early groundwork reduce risk, but if issues emerge, you must act quickly to redesign routes or replace defective sections. The golden rule is simple: respond, don’t react. Investigate the issue, gather expert input, quantify the impact, and communicate clearly with your contractor, lender, and investors. When you handle unforeseen issues with professionalism and composure, you maintain control and the project stays on track.

Chapter 12: Risk Management; Anticipating, Assessing, and Controlling Development Risks

12.1 Structural Risk

Structural risk is one of the most serious threats in any commercial-to-residential conversion. Older commercial buildings often hide decades of wear, undocumented alterations, and hidden weaknesses that only become visible once work begins. If structural issues are not identified early, they can derail timelines, inflate costs, and in extreme cases make a project unviable. Professional developers treat structural risk as a priority, not an afterthought.

The first danger lies in load-bearing elements. Many commercial buildings have been modified repeatedly over the years, walls removed, beams added, floors strengthened or weakened. What appears to be a simple partition wall may be carrying significant load. Misjudging this can lead to unsafe demolition, costly redesigns, or emergency structural interventions. Early structural surveys and intrusive investigations reduce this risk dramatically.

Roof integrity is another common issue. Flat roofs, ageing trusses, water ingress, and hidden rot can compromise the building's stability. A failing roof affects insulation, fire safety, and long-term durability. Replacing or strengthening a roof is expensive, so understanding its condition early is essential for accurate budgeting and lender confidence. Subsidence and ground movement also pose significant risks. Older commercial buildings may sit on inadequate foundations, especially if they were originally designed for light industrial or office use. Cracks, uneven floors, or distorted frames can indicate deeper structural problems. A structural engineer must assess these signs before you commit to the purchase.

Fire compartmentation failures are another hidden danger. Many commercial buildings lack the fire-rated walls, floors, and penetrations required for residential use. Rectifying compartmentation issues can be complex and costly, especially once services and layouts are installed. Structural risk does not disappear by ignoring it. It must be identified early, quantified accurately, and managed professionally. When you understand the building's true condition before committing to the deal, you protect your budget, your timeline, and your reputation and you dramatically increase the likelihood of a successful conversion.

12.2 Planning and Policy Risk

Planning and policy risk is one of the most unpredictable elements in commercial-to-residential development. Unlike structural or financial risks, which can be quantified with surveys and cost plans, planning risk is influenced by human judgement, political priorities, and evolving regulations. A project that appears viable today can become challenging tomorrow if local policy shifts or national rules tighten. Professional developers anticipate these uncertainties and build strategies that remain resilient under changing conditions.

The first major risk is planning decisions themselves. Even under Prior Approval routes such as Class MA, outcomes are not guaranteed. Local authorities may challenge transport impact, natural light compliance, contamination, or noise exposure. A refusal can delay the project, increase costs, or force a redesign. Early engagement with a planning consultant reduces this risk by identifying potential objections before submission. Local policy shifts also create uncertainty. Councils regularly update their Local Plans, introduce new design guides, or tighten expectations around housing mix, amenity space, or sustainability. A scheme that aligned with policy last year may face new requirements today. Staying informed and submitting applications promptly helps protect your position.

Article 4 Directions are another significant risk. These remove permitted development rights in specific areas, often town centres or high-street zones where councils want to protect commercial stock. If Article 4 is proposed, developers must act quickly; once confirmed, it can eliminate the viability of a conversion entirely.

Political and regulatory changes add further complexity. National planning reforms, building-regulation updates, and shifts in government priorities can affect timelines, costs, and feasibility. Developers who rely solely on current rules without considering future changes expose themselves to unnecessary risk. Planning and policy risk cannot be eliminated, but it can be managed. With strong consultants, proactive research, and flexible design strategies, you can navigate uncertainty and keep your project aligned with both current and emerging requirements.

12.3 Cost Overrun Risk

Cost overrun risk is one of the most common and most damaging threats in commercial-to-residential development. Even a well-planned project can experience budget pressure from material inflation, labor shortages, unforeseen work, or design changes. Developers who fail to anticipate these risks often see their profit eroded long before the project reaches completion. Effective cost management is not about luck; it is about discipline, foresight, and control.

One of the biggest drivers of cost overruns is material inflation. Prices for timber, steel, plasterboard, and M&E components can fluctuate rapidly, especially during periods of economic uncertainty. If your cost plan is based on outdated prices or optimistic assumptions, you may face significant increases once procurement begins. Locking in prices early and working with suppliers who offer fixed-term quotes reduces this risk.

Labor shortages also contribute to rising costs. Skilled trades may be in high demand, leading to premium rates or delays that extend preliminaries and overheads. Developers must assess contractor capacity, avoid over-stretched teams, and ensure the programme is realistic. Variations are another major source of cost escalation. These arise from design changes, unclear drawings, or unexpected discoveries during strip-out. Without strict variation control pricing before approval, written sign-off, and cumulative tracking variations can quietly consume your contingency.

Unforeseen works, such as structural defects, drainage failures, or compliance upgrades, can also disrupt budgets. While some surprises are unavoidable, early surveys, intrusive investigations, and strong due diligence significantly reduce the likelihood of major shocks.

The final risk is poor financial discipline. Developers who make impulsive upgrades, accept vague contractor quotes, or fail to monitor valuations often lose control of their budget. Cost overrun risk cannot be eliminated, but it can be managed. With accurate cost planning, disciplined monitoring, and proactive decision-making, you protect your margin and maintain a financially resilient project.

12.4 Market and Exit Risk

Market and exit risk is one of the most overlooked yet critical elements of commercial-to-residential development. A project can be structurally sound, well-designed, and efficiently delivered but if the market shifts at the wrong moment, profitability can evaporate. Professional developers plan for uncertainty by analyzing demand, monitoring economic trends, and building flexible exit strategies that protect their position.

The first major risk is rental demand. Local employment trends, transport links, and demographic shifts all influence how quickly units will let and at what price. Overestimating rental values or absorption rates can lead to cash-flow pressure, extended voids, and reduced returns. Early market research, comparable analysis, and conversations with local agents help anchor assumptions in reality.

Sales values carry similar uncertainty. GDV risk increases when interest rates rise, mortgage affordability tightens, or buyer sentiment weakens. A strong sales market can turn quickly, especially in areas reliant on first-time buyers or investor purchasers. Developers must stress-test their GDV against conservative scenarios to ensure the project remains viable even in softer conditions. Lender appetite also fluctuates. Banks may tighten criteria, reduce loan-to-value ratios, or increase stress-testing requirements. This can affect both development finance and exit refinancing. Developers who rely on a single lender or assume favourable terms without contingency expose themselves to

unnecessary risk.
Interest rate changes amplify all other risks. Higher rates increase development finance costs, reduce investor appetite, and suppress buyer affordability. A project that looked profitable at 5% of finance may struggle at 8%. The strongest defense against market and exit risk is multiple exit strategies.

A scheme should be able to:
- *Sell units individually*
- *Sell in bulk to an investor*
- *Refinance and hold as a rental asset*
- *Convert to a different tenure if needed (e.g., serviced accommodation, co-living, HMOs where compliant)*

When you design your project with flexibility and resilience, you protect your profitability regardless of market conditions.

12.5 Legal and Compliance Risk

Legal and compliance risk is one of the most underestimated threats in commercial-to-residential development. A project can be financially strong and structurally sound yet still collapse under the weight of legal complications. Title defects, restrictive covenants, easements, AML obligations, and defective documentation can all create delays, disputes, or even make a scheme unviable. Professional developers treat legal due diligence as a core part of risk management not a box-ticking exercise.
One of the most common issues is title defects. These may include missing rights of access, unclear ownership boundaries, unregistered land, or unresolved charges. If not identified early, title problems can delay funding, block planning, or prevent future sales. A thorough title review by a competent solicitor is essential before committing to the purchase. Restrictive covenants and easements pose additional risks. A covenant may prohibit residential use, limit alterations, or restrict development density. Easements such as rights of way, shared access, or utility routes can limit design options or reduce the site's value. These issues must be understood and costed before you finalize your

strategy.

AML compliance is another critical area. Developers must verify investor identity, confirm source of funds, and maintain accurate records. Failure to comply can lead to penalties, delays, or frozen transactions. AML is not optional; it is a legal requirement that protects both the developer and the wider market. Defective or incomplete documentation also creates risk. Missing warranties, outdated fire reports, incomplete leases, or inaccurate plans can lead to disputes with contractors, lenders, or future buyers. Developers must ensure that all documentation is accurate, current, and professionally prepared.

Legal and compliance risk cannot be eliminated, but it can be controlled. With strong solicitors, early due diligence, and disciplined documentation, you avoid costly disputes and keep your project legally robust from acquisition to exit.

12.6 Practical Mitigation Strategies and Contingency Planning

Risk management is not about eliminating uncertainty, it is about preparing for it. Every commercial-to-residential conversion carries structural, financial, legal, and market risks. The developers who succeed consistently are those who build robust mitigation strategies and contingency plans long before problems arise. A risk-aware mindset protects the project, the investor, and your reputation.

The first step is stress-testing the deal. This means modelling conservative scenarios for GDV, build costs, interest rates, and programme duration. If the project only works under perfect conditions, it is not a resilient deal. A strong appraisal should remain viable even with reduced values, increased costs, or extended timelines. Next is building contingencies. A realistic contingency allowance typically 10–15% for conversions protect you from unforeseen works, variations, and inflation. Contingency is not a luxury; it is a financial safety net that prevents panic decisions when surprises emerge.

Contract structure is another powerful mitigation tool. Fixed-price contracts, milestone-based payments, clear variation procedures, and retention clauses all reduce exposure to cost overruns and disputes. A well-written contract is one of the strongest forms of risk control.

Managing professionals effectively also reduces risk. Early engagement with structural engineers, planning consultants, M&E designers, and building control ensures that problems are identified before they become expensive. Regular coordination meetings keep everyone aligned and reduce the likelihood of design clashes or compliance failures.

A risk-aware developer also maintains multiple exit strategies. Whether the market shifts, lenders tighten criteria, or sales slow, you must be able to pivot refinance, hold, sell individually, or sell in bulk. Flexibility is a form of protection.

Finally, cultivate a mindset of proactive communication. Investors, lenders, and contractors respond well to clarity, honesty, and early warnings. Silence creates risk; transparency builds trust. When you combine stress-testing, contingencies, strong contracts, expert management, and flexible exits, you create a development strategy that can withstand uncertainty and still deliver profitable, predictable outcomes.

Chapter 13: Build-to-Rent vs Build-to-Sell

13.1 Rental Yields vs Capital Gains

One of the defining decisions in any development strategy is whether to hold a complete scheme for rental income or sell it to realize capital gains. Both approaches can be highly profitable, but they serve different financial goals, risk profiles, and time horizons.
Understanding the dynamics of rental yields versus capital gains allows developers to choose the strategy that best aligns with their objectives and market conditions.

Rental yields represent the ongoing income generated by the property. They are calculated by dividing annual rental income by the property's value, giving a percentage return. Strong yields provide predictable cash flow, support long-term wealth building, and create resilience during market downturns. Build to Rent strategies appeal to investors seeking stability, passive income, and long-term asset growth. They also benefit from refinancing opportunities, allowing developers to recycle capital while retaining ownership.

Capital gains, on the other hand, are realized when the property is sold at a higher value than its cost. This approach focuses on maximizing GDV, delivering a lump-sum profit, and freeing capital for the next project. Build to Sell strategies suit developers who prioritize speed of return, higher short-term profits, and rapid scaling. However, they are more exposed to market cycles, buyer sentiment, and interest rate fluctuations. Market conditions heavily influence which strategy is optimal. In high-interest-rate environments, rental demand often strengthens as fewer people can buy, improving yields. In strong sales markets with rising values, capital gains become more attractive. A sophisticated developer evaluates both paths and stress-tests the project under multiple scenarios.

Ultimately, the choice between renting and selling is not binary. The strongest developers design schemes with dual exit potential, allowing them to pivot based on market performance. Flexibility protects profitability and ensures the project remains viable regardless of economic shifts.

13.2. Holding for Cash Flow vs Selling for Lump Sums

Every developer eventually faces a strategic choice: hold the completed units for long-term cash flow or sell them to release a lump-sum profit. Both paths can be highly effective, but they serve different financial needs, risk appetites, and stages of an investor's journey. Understanding the distinction is essential for building a sustainable, scalable property business.

Holding for cash flow priorities long-term income and asset growth. Monthly rental income provides predictable cash flow, supports financial stability, and strengthens borrowing capacity for future projects. Over time, rental assets benefit from capital appreciation, mortgage pay-down, and inflation-linked rent increases. This strategy suits investors who value stability, passive income, and long-term wealth creation. It is especially powerful for those building a portfolio designed to replace employment income or create generational wealth. Selling for lump sums, by contrast, focuses on immediate capital release. A successful sale delivers a large profit that can be reinvested quickly into new projects, enabling faster scaling and higher annual returns. This approach suits developers who prioritize liquidity, rapid growth, or short-term profit cycles. However, it exposes the investor to market timing, buyer sentiment, and sales-related risks. Liquidity needs to play a major role in the decision. Investors with limited capital may prefer selling to recycle funds, while those with strong cash reserves may choose to hold and compound long-term returns. Portfolio maturity also matters early-stage investors often sell to build momentum, while established investors increasingly hold to stabilize income.

Risk appetite is another key factor. Holding reduces exposure to market volatility but ties up capital. Selling increases liquidity but relies on favorable market conditions. The most sophisticated developers design schemes with dual-exit flexibility. By ensuring the project works both as a rental asset and a sales product, they can pivot based on market performance protecting profitability and long-term strategy.

13.3 Refinancing Options After Completion

Refinancing is one of the most powerful tools available to a developer after completing a commercial-to-residential conversion. When used strategically, it allows you to recycle capital, improve cash flow, and accelerate portfolio growth without relying solely on sales. Understanding how refinancing works and how lenders assess risk is essential for building a sustainable development business.

The foundation of refinancing is valuation uplift. Once the conversion is complete, the property is valued based on its new residential use, rental income, and comparable sales. This uplift creates equity that can be released through refinancing. The stronger the design, finish, and rental demand, the higher the valuation and the more capital you can extract. Lenders assess refinancing applications using specific criteria. One of the most important is the Interest Coverage Ratio (ICR), which measures whether the rental income comfortably covers the mortgage payments. Higher interest rates or lower rents reduce the ICR, limiting how much you can borrow. Developers must ensure their rental assumptions are realistic and supported by local comparables. Lenders also apply stress testing, modelling higher interest rates to ensure the loan remains affordable under adverse conditions. A project that works at today's rates may fail under stress-tested scenarios, so developers must plan conservatively.

Refinancing options vary. Traditional buy-to-let mortgages suit single units, while portfolio loans, commercial mortgages, and specialist BTR products suit multi-unit schemes. Some lenders offer bridge-to-term products, allowing a seamless transition from development finance to long-term debt. The primary benefit of refinancing is the ability to recycle capital. By extracting equity, you can repay investors, reduce personal exposure, or fund the next project all while retaining ownership of the asset and its long-term income.

Refinancing is not guaranteed. It requires strong documentation, compliant construction, stable rental demand, and a well-presented asset. But when executed correctly, it transforms a single project into a scalable, long-term investment engine.

13.4 Portfolio Strategy: When to Keep, When to Sell

A successful property career is not built on individual projects alone it is built on the strategic decisions that determine which assets you keep and which you sell. Knowing when to hold and when to exit is one of the most important skills a developer can master. These decisions shape liquidity, risk exposure, long-term income, and the overall resilience of your portfolio.

The first consideration is market timing. In rising markets, selling can accelerate capital growth and free funds for new opportunities. In softer markets, holding may be wiser, allowing you to benefit from stable rental income while waiting for values to recover. A disciplined investor avoids emotional decisions and relies on data: comparable sales, rental trends, interest rate forecasts, and local economic indicators.

Asset performance is equally important. High-yielding units in strong rental locations often make excellent long-term holds, especially when they deliver consistent cash flow and low voids. Conversely, assets with weaker yields, high maintenance costs, or limited long-term upside may be better candidates for disposal. Selling underperforming assets strengthens the overall health of the portfolio.

Geographic considerations also influence strategy. Concentrated portfolios can deliver management efficiency, but they also increase exposure to local economic shifts. Diversifying across regions or even across asset classes can reduce risk and stabilize long-term returns.

Portfolio maturity plays a major role. Early-stage investors often sell more frequently to build capital quickly. As the portfolio grows, the emphasis typically shifts toward holding assets that provide stable income and long-term appreciation. Mature portfolios prioritize resilience over rapid recycling.

The strongest investors adopt a balanced approach: holding assets that deliver dependable cash flow while selling selectively to release capital for new opportunities. This balance creates a portfolio that is both profitable and adaptable capable of thriving through market cycles and supporting long-term wealth creation.

13.5 Tax and Long-Term Wealth Considerations (High-Level, non-Advisory)

Tax plays a significant role in shaping long-term wealth outcomes for property investors. While specific tax planning requires personalized professional advice, every developer should understand the high-level implications of different exit strategies. The way you structure your deals, hold your assets, and plan your exits can influence how much wealth you retain over time.

For investors who hold assets for rental income, the primary consideration is rental income tax. Rental profits are typically taxed annually, meaning cash flow must be strong enough to cover both mortgage payments and tax liabilities. Over time, rising rents and stable debt can create increasing net income, supporting long-term wealth accumulation. Investors often explore efficient ownership structures to manage tax exposure, but these decisions must be made with professional guidance.

For those who sell assets, Capital Gains Tax (CGT) becomes relevant. When a property is sold for more than its base cost, the gain may be taxable. The timing of the sale, ownership structure, and available allowances can all influence the final tax position. Developers who rely on Build to Sell strategies must factor CGT into their profit calculations to avoid overestimating returns. Long-term investors also consider inheritance planning. Property is a significant asset class in many estates, and its value can create future tax implications for beneficiaries. High-level strategies such as gifting, trusts, or corporate structures may play a role in long-term planning, but these require specialist advice to implement correctly.

Chapter 14: Making the Right Offers Consistently

14.1 Start with the End in Mind: GDV, Demand and Viability

Every successful offer begins long before numbers are placed on the table. Professional developers understand that the true anchor of any acquisition is the Gross Development Value, not the asking price. GDV represents the realistic value of the completed scheme, and it is the single most important figure in the entire appraisal. When calculated properly, it becomes the compass that guides every financial decision, every negotiation, and ultimately the offer itself.

A reliable GDV is built on evidence rather than optimism. This means studying comparable sales, analyzing rental demand, and understanding the absorption rate of similar units in the area. A building that appears attractive at first glance may produce apartments that are misaligned with local demand too small, too large, or simply unsuitable for the demographic that actually buys or rents in that location. If the end product is wrong, the GDV will be wrong, and if the GDV is wrong, the offer will inevitably be wrong. This is why disciplined developers begin with the finished scheme in mind, not the seller's expectations.

Understanding the end also requires clarity around exit strategy. A scheme intended for individual sales will be valued differently from one held for rental income. Bulk sales, refinancing, and long-term holds each come with their own valuation methods, lender criteria, and risk profiles. The exit you choose shapes the GDV you rely on, and your offer must reflect the exit that is most realistic for the building, the market, and your wider portfolio strategy. Starting with the end in mind removes emotion from the process. It forces you to anchor your assumptions in reality and prevents you from chasing deals that cannot deliver. When GDV becomes your guiding reference point, your offers become sharper, safer, and consistently aligned with the true potential of the finished scheme

14.2 Build a Conservative Cost Plan and Stress-Test the Deal

Once GDV is established, the next step is to build a conservative, fully-loaded cost plan. Commercial conversions are notorious for hidden costs: structural surprises, compliance upgrades, M&E redesigns, and professional fees that escalate as the project evolves.

Your cost plan must include:

- *Construction costs*
- *Professional fees*
- *Finance costs*
- *Contingency (10–15%)*
- *Planning or Prior Approval fees*
- *Compliance upgrades (fire, acoustic, drainage, insulation)*
- *Risk allowances for unknowns*

Then comes the stress test. A strong deal must survive:

- *Higher interest rates*
- *Lower GDV*
- *Longer programme*
- *Increased build costs*

If the deal collapses under conservative assumptions, it is not a deal. Stress-testing protects you from overpaying and ensures your offer is grounded in reality, not hope.

A robust cost plan accounts for every major category of expenditure. Construction costs must be based on realistic contractor pricing rather than assumptions. Professional fees should reflect the full team required to deliver the scheme, including architects, engineers, planning consultants, building control, and specialist assessors. Finance costs must be calculated with accuracy, acknowledging that interest accumulates throughout the programme. Contingency is not optional; it is a protective buffer that absorbs the inevitable surprises that arise during strip-out and construction. Compliance upgrades, from fire safety to acoustic performance and drainage improvements, must also be included, as these are common areas where commercial buildings fall short of residential standards. Finally, allowances for unknown risks ensure that the appraisal remains resilient even when unexpected issues emerge.

Once the cost plan is complete, the deal must be stress-tested. A strong project should remain viable even when conditions worsen. This means modelling scenarios where interest rates rise, GDV softens, the programme extends, or build costs increase. If the numbers collapse under these conservative assumptions, the deal is not strong enough to proceed. Stress-testing protects you from overpaying and prevents you from committing to a project that only works in perfect conditions. It forces discipline, sharpens your offer, and ensures that your appraisal is grounded in reality rather than hope.

14.3 Calculate Your Maximum Allowable Offer (MAO)

With the Gross Development Value (GDV) and costs established, you can calculate your Maximum Allowable Offer (MAO) the highest price you can pay while still achieving your required profit.

The formula is simple:
MAO = GDV – Total Costs – Required Profit

Professional developers work backwards from a minimum acceptable profit margin, typically:

- *20% on GDV, or*
- *25–30% on cost*

This margin protects you from risk, market shifts, and unforeseen works. If the seller's expectations exceed your MAO, you walk away. The wrong deal is worse than no deal.

MAO is not a negotiation tactic it is a financial boundary. It keeps you disciplined, unemotional, and consistent. When you know your MAO, you never overpay, and you never justify a bad deal.

How to Calculate Gross Development Value (GDV)

You calculate GDV by adding up the realistic market value of each completed unit.

For example:

• *If you convert a commercial building into 6 flats*
• *And each flat will sell for £250,000*

Then:

GDV = £250,000 × 6 = £1,500,000

That £1.5 million is the number you use to:

• *Stress-test the deal*
• *Calculate your maximum offer*
• *Determine your borrowing capacity*
• *Assess your profit margin*

14.4 Presenting Offers Professionally and Making Them Consistently

The final step is execution. Even the best offer fails if it is presented poorly. Agents and sellers respond to clarity, confidence, and professionalism.

A strong offer includes:

• *A clear rationale*
• *Evidence-based GDV*
• *A conservative cost plan*
• *Proof of funds or lender support*
• *A realistic timeline*
• *A confident, concise explanation of your approach*

Professional presentation often beats higher offers because it builds trust and reduces perceived risk.
Consistency is equally important.

The developers who secure the best deals are the ones who:

• *Analyze more buildings*
• *Make more offers*

• *Follow a repeatable system*
• *Stay emotionally detached*
• *Track outcomes and refine their process*

Offer-making is a numbers game but only if the numbers are correct.
A strong offer is built on a clear rationale. When you explain how you arrived at your number, referencing comparable evidence, realistic GDV assumptions, and a conservative cost plan, you shift the conversation from emotion to logic. Sellers may not agree with your figure, but they will respect the reasoning behind it. Providing proof of funds or lender support reinforces your credibility, while outlining a realistic timeline shows that you understand the practical steps required to complete the deal. A concise explanation of your approach communicates confidence without overselling, and this often carries more weight than a higher but uncertain offer.

Professional presentation frequently outperforms higher bids because it reduces perceived risk. Sellers want certainty, and agents want a smooth transaction. When you present yourself as the buyer who understands the process, communicates clearly, and moves decisively, you become the preferred option even if your offer is not the highest on the table.

Consistency is equally important. The developers who secure the best deals are those who analyze more buildings, make more offers, and follow a repeatable system. They remain emotionally detached, allowing the numbers to guide their decisions rather than excitement or pressure. They also track their outcomes, learning from each offer and refining their approach over time. Offer-making is ultimately a numbers game, but only when the numbers are correct and the process is consistent.

14.5 Common Offer-Making Mistakes to Avoid

Most failed deals don't collapse because the building was wrong they collapse because the developer made avoidable mistakes during the offer stage. Understanding these pitfalls helps you stay disciplined, protect your margin, and maintain credibility with agents and sellers.

One of the most common mistakes is starting with the asking price instead of the numbers. Emotional buyers anchor themselves to what the seller wants, rather than what the deal can support. Professional developers ignore the asking price entirely until the MAO is calculated. Another mistake is underestimating costs. Developers often rely on optimistic build estimates, incomplete surveys, or outdated contractor quotes. Commercial conversions always reveal surprises asbestos, drainage issues, structural defects, fire compliance upgrades and failing to price these in leads to overpaying.

A third mistake is overestimating GDV. Inflated comparables, unrealistic rental assumptions, or ignoring absorption rates can distort the entire appraisal. A small GDV error can wipe out your profit.

Developers also fail when they don't stress-test. If your offer only works under perfect conditions, it's not a deal it's a gamble.

Another major pitfall is ignoring risk. Planning uncertainty, title issues, and structural unknowns must be priced into the offer. If risk isn't reflected in the number, you're paying retail for a wholesale opportunity.

Finally, many developers don't make enough offers. They analyze endlessly, hesitate, or wait for the "perfect" deal. Consistency beats perfection. The more offers you make, the more deals you secure.

Avoiding these mistakes keeps your offer process sharp, disciplined, and profitable.

14.6 Negotiation Strategies for Commercial Conversions

Negotiation in commercial conversions is not about pressure or persuasion, it's about clarity, confidence, and professionalism. Sellers respond to certainty, not charm. Your goal is to demonstrate that you are the safest, most reliable buyer, even if your offer is not the highest.

The strongest negotiation strategy is evidence-based communication. When you present your offer with comparables, cost plans, and a clear rationale, you shift the conversation from emotion to logic. Sellers trust buyers who can explain their numbers calmly and confidently.

Another powerful strategy is framing your offer around risk. Commercial buildings carry structural, planning, and compliance uncertainties. When you explain that your offer reflects these risks and that you are absorbing them sellers understand why your number is realistic. Speed and certainty are also negotiation tools. Agents value buyers who can move quickly, provide proof of funds, and demonstrate a clear process. A lower offer with high certainty often beats a higher offer with uncertainty.

You should also use silence strategically. Once you present your offer, stop talking. Let the agent or seller respond. Overexplaining weakens your position. Another key strategy is walking away professionally. When you calmly withdraw because the numbers don't work, you signal discipline and seriousness. Agents remember this and they call you first when a deal falls through or a seller becomes realistic.

Finally, negotiation is strengthened by consistency. When you make offers regularly, agents begin to trust your process, your numbers, and your reliability. Over time, this reputation becomes one of your strongest negotiation advantages.

Conclusion

Commercial conversion is no longer a fringe strategy reserved for seasoned developers or opportunistic investors. It has become a structural shift in how the United Kingdom uses its buildings, reimagines its high streets, and responds to the evolving needs of its people. The old model where commercial spaces thrived on footfall, retail demand, and office occupancy has been permanently disrupted. In its place stands a new reality: a nation with an oversupply of outdated commercial stock and an undersupply of quality homes. This imbalance is not a temporary market quirk; it is a long-term transformation that will define property investment for decades.

The investors who succeed in this new landscape are not simply those with the deepest pockets or the most experience. They are the ones who can see potential where others see decline. They are the ones who walk past an empty shop and imagine a pair of modern flats. They look at a tired office block and see the outline of future apartments. They understand that a pub with a fading sign and boarded windows may be the foundation of a thriving co-living space. Commercial conversion is, at its core, a creative discipline a blend of vision, analysis, and execution

But creativity alone is not enough. Success in this field requires planning agility, financial discipline, and a deep respect for compliance. The rules governing commercial-to-residential conversion are powerful, but they are also precise. Class MA opens doors, but it does not eliminate the need for due diligence. Prior Approval is faster than full planning, but it still demands clarity, documentation, and a strong understanding of local policy. Building regulations are non-negotiable, and fire safety is paramount. The investors who thrive are those who embrace these constraints as part of the craft, not obstacles to be avoided.

Financial discipline is equally essential. Commercial conversion can deliver exceptional returns, but only when approached with rigor.

Budgets must be realistic; contingencies must be built in and exit strategies must be clear from the outset. The most successful investors are those who understand the numbers intimately who can run a back-of-the-envelope appraisal in minutes but also know when to bring in specialists for deeper analysis. They understand bridging finance, development finance, GDV-based lending, and the psychology of private investors. They know how to present deals professionally, communicate risks transparently, and build long-term funding relationships based on trust.

Yet beyond the planning rules and financial models lies something even more important: the ability to see "homes" where others see "empty shops." This mindset is what separates the opportunist from the visionary. It is what allows an investor to walk into a cold, echoing commercial unit and imagine the warmth of a finished living space. It is what transforms a derelict building into a place where people can build their lives, raise families, and contribute to the community. Commercial conversion is not just about profit; it is about regeneration. It is about breathing life back into forgotten buildings and neglected streets.

As the economy stabilizes and the demand for quality housing continues to rise, the investors who master commercial conversion will hold some of the most resilient and valuable portfolios in the country. Residential demand is not going away. People will always need homes homes that are well-designed, energy-efficient, and located in the heart of communities. Commercial conversion delivers exactly that. It creates homes where infrastructure already exists, where transport links are established, and where amenities are within walking distance. It aligns perfectly with the government's long-term vision for sustainable, compact, community-focused development.

Moreover, commercial conversion offers resilience in a way few other strategies can. It is resilient to inflation, because rents rise with the cost of living. It is resilient to recession, because people do not stop needing homes. It is resilient to unemployment, because mid-market residential units remain in demand even when incomes fluctuate. It is resilient to planning uncertainty, because PDR provides a clear, structured pathway for transformation. And it is resilient to market volatility, because the value created through conversion is based on real, tangible improvement not speculation.

This book has given you the frameworks, the strategies, and the insights needed to navigate this powerful opportunity. You now understand the planning landscape, the financial structures, the legal agreements, the compliance requirements, and the project management principles that underpin successful conversions. You have learned how to source buildings, appraise deals, manage risk, and execute with confidence. You have seen how to think like a developer, negotiate like a professional, and build like a strategist.

But knowledge alone is not enough. The real transformation happens when you take action when you walk into your first commercial building with a new set of eyes, when you run your first feasibility check, when you speak to your first commercial agent with confidence, when you submit your first Prior Approval application, when you raise your first round of investor finance, and when you stand in your first completed conversion knowing that you turned potential into reality.

Commercial conversion is not just a strategy. It is a mindset. It is a way of seeing the world differently of recognizing that every empty building is a story waiting to be rewritten. And for those who embrace this mindset, the future is full of opportunity.

Real-Life Commercial Conversions

Real-life examples bring theory to life. They show what is possible, what can go wrong, and what separates a smooth project from a stressful one. The following case studies are based on common patterns seen across the UK market not tied to any specific investor, but grounded in realistic numbers, timelines, and challenges. Each one illustrates a different type of commercial building, a different planning route, and a different exit strategy. Together, they demonstrate the versatility and power of commercial conversion when executed with clarity, discipline, and vision.

Case Study 1: Small Shop to Two Flats

A tired corner shop in a suburban high street is one of the most common and most accessible commercial conversion opportunities. In this example, the shop had been vacant for nearly two years. The owner, a retired shopkeeper, was motivated to sell. The building consisted of a ground-floor retail unit with a large storage area at the back and a disused loft above. The structure was sound, the frontage was dated, and the layout was inefficient perfect conditions for a value-add conversion.

Numbers:

The shop was purchased for £145,000. A quick feasibility check suggested it could be converted into two one-bed flats: one on the ground floor and one in the loft space. The build cost was estimated at £95,000, including a new roof, insulation upgrades, fire separation, and full internal reconfiguration. Total project cost, including finance and professional fees, came to around £260,000. The end value (GDV) was £330,000 based on local comparables.

Timeline:

The project took nine months from acquisition to completion. Prior Approval under Class MA was granted in eight weeks. The build phase lasted five months, with an additional month for snagging, certification, and refinancing.

Challenges:

The biggest challenge was natural light. The rear of the shop had no windows, so the design required creative solutions: lightwells, rooflights, and internal reconfiguration to ensure habitable rooms met daylight standards. Another challenge was the loft conversion, which required strengthening the floor and adding dormers to create usable space. These changes increased costs but also improved the final value.

Lessons:

This project highlighted the importance of early design thinking. A small building can feel cramped if poorly planned, but spacious if the layout is optimized. It also reinforced the value of strong relationships with building control; early engagement prevented delays later. Finally, it demonstrated that small conversions could deliver strong returns when purchased at the right price and executed with precision.

Case Study 2: Office Block to Apartments

A three-storey office block on the edge of a town centre represents a more ambitious conversion. Built in the 1980s, the building had open-plan floors, suspended ceilings, and outdated mechanical systems. It had been partially vacant for years as businesses moved to modern co-working spaces. The structure was solid, the floor plates were generous, and the location was close to transport links ideal conditions for residential conversion.

Numbers:

The building was purchased for £725,000. The plan was to convert it into 12 apartments: eight one-bed units and four studios. The build cost was £780,000, including new windows, fire compartment, acoustic upgrades, and a full M&E overhaul. Total project cost reached £1.65 million. The GDV was £2.25 million based on local sales values.

Planning Journey:

The project proceeded under Class MA, but the council requested additional information on transport impact, noise mitigation, and waste storage. A robust Prior Approval package was submitted, including acoustic reports and a daylight/sunlight assessment. Approval was granted in 10 weeks. No external alterations were required, which kept the process streamlined.

Finance Structure:

The acquisition was funded with a bridging loan at 70% LTV. Development finance covered 100% of build costs, drawn down in stages. The investor contributed £300,000 in equity. Upon completion, the building was refinanced on a long-term buy-to-let product at 75% LTV, releasing £1.68 million enough to repay all lenders and return most of the investor's capital.

Challenges:

The biggest challenge was fire safety. The building required a protected stair core, upgraded fire doors, and a new alarm system. The second challenge was acoustic performance; offices are not designed for residential noise separation. Additional insulation and floating floors were required. These issues increased costs but were essential for compliance.

Lessons:
This project demonstrated the importance of professional reports. Acoustic engineers, fire consultants, and M&E designers played critical roles. It also showed how GDV-based lending can unlock larger projects by leveraging the uplift created through conversion. Finally, it reinforced the need for contingency funds; unexpected upgrades are common in older office buildings.

Case Study 3: Pub to HMO or Co-Living

Pubs are iconic British buildings full of character, history, and community significance. But many have struggled in recent years, leaving behind large, underused spaces. In this example, a two-storey pub on a residential street had closed three years earlier. The ground floor was a large open bar area, while the upper floor contained former staff accommodation. The building had charm, generous ceiling heights, and a central location ideal for co-living.

Community Impact:
Before proceeding, the investor engaged with local residents. Some were sad to see the pub go, but many welcomed the idea of revitalizing a derelict building. The investor proposed a co-living scheme with communal spaces, high-quality design, and strict management standards. This approach aligned with local housing needs and reduced resistance.

Design Choices:
The ground floor was reconfigured into a shared kitchen, dining area, and lounge. The upper floor was converted into six en-suite bedrooms. The design preserved original features exposed beams, brickwork, and the old fireplace blending heritage with modern living. Energy

efficiency upgrades included insulation, new windows, and efficient heating systems.

Risk Management:
Pubs often come with hidden risks. In this case, asbestos was discovered in the ceiling voids, requiring specialist removal. The drainage system also needed upgrading to handle multiple en-suite bathrooms. Fire safety was a major focus: the building required a full alarm system, fire doors, and compartmentation. These issues increased costs but were managed through contingency planning.

Lessons:
This project showed the importance of community engagement, especially when converting buildings with emotional significance. It also highlighted the need for thorough surveys; pubs often hide surprises. Finally, it demonstrated the potential of co-living as a modern housing solution one that blends affordability, community, and design.

Appendix: Building Your Power Team

1. Specialist Solicitor (Commercial Titles, Overage, Covenants)

A specialist solicitor is the backbone of any commercial conversion project. Unlike residential conveyancing, commercial titles often contain layers of complexity: restrictive covenants, overage clauses, rights of access, historic easements, and unusual lease structures. A solicitor who understands commercial property law can identify risks early, negotiate amendments, and ensure the title you are buying is fit for conversion. Their expertise protects you from hidden liabilities and prevents costly legal disputes later. In commercial conversion, the solicitor is not just a box-ticking professional they are your first line of defense.

2. Commercial Estate Agent (Off-Market and Distressed Deals)

Commercial agents operate in a different world from residential agents. They speak the language of yields, leases, footfall, and business viability. They also hold the keys to off-market opportunities, distressed assets, and buildings that never reach public listings. Building a strong relationship with a commercial agent can unlock deals long before competitors see them. When treated as long-term partners rather than transactional intermediaries, these agents become invaluable sources of insight, opportunity, and negotiation leverage.

3. RICS Surveyor & Structural Engineer

Technical due diligence is essential in commercial conversion. A RICS surveyor provides a detailed assessment of the building's condition, highlighting defects, maintenance issues, and potential risks. A structural engineer goes deeper, examining load-bearing walls, foundations, roof integrity, and the building's capacity to support new layouts. Their reports guide your feasibility analysis, inform your design decisions, and help you avoid structural surprises that could derail the project. Together, they ensure you understand exactly what you are buying before you commit.

4. Planning Consultant

A planning consultant is your navigator through the complex world of planning policy. They interpret local regulations, advise on the best planning route, prepare Prior Approval or full planning applications, and communicate with the council on your behalf. A skilled consultant can anticipate objections, prepare robust documentation, and align your proposal with local priorities. Their involvement can save months of delay and significantly increase your chances of approval. In commercial conversion, planning strategy is everything and your consultant is the strategist.

5. Quantity Surveyor (QS)

A quantity surveyor provides financial clarity and cost control throughout the project. They prepare detailed cost plans, monitor spending, manage variations, and ensure the building remains within budget. Their discipline protects your margins and prevents budget creeping in. This is one of the most common risks in commercial conversion. A good QS becomes the financial conscience of the project, ensuring every decision is grounded in numbers, not assumptions.

6. Accountant and Tax Advisor

Your accountant and tax advisor help structure your business, manage cash flow, and plan for long-term wealth. They ensure your company setup, VAT treatment, and financial reporting align with your goals and obligations. They also help you understand the tax implications of different exit strategies, refinancing decisions, and portfolio structures. While they do not provide personalized tax advice within this book, their role in your real-world team is essential for long-term sustainability.

7. Mortgage Broker / Finance Specialist

A finance specialist connects you to the right lenders at every stage of the project. They understand bridging finance, development loans, GDV-based lending, and long-term refinancing options. Their relationships with lenders can unlock better terms, faster approvals, and more flexible structures. They also help you present your project professionally, ensuring lenders see you as a credible, capable developer. In commercial conversion, finance is the engine and your broker is the engineer who keeps it running smoothly.

What to Do Next: A Practical Roadmap

a. Choose Your Investment Area

Begin by selecting a location where commercial-to-residential conversion is both viable and profitable. Research local rental demand, sales values, vacancy rates, and the types of commercial buildings available. Look for high streets with tired shops, office clusters with declining occupancy, and mixed-use areas undergoing regeneration. The right area combines affordability, strong demand for housing, and buildings with genuine conversion potential.

b. Build Your Power Team

Before analyzing deals, assemble the professionals who will support your journey. This includes a commercial-savvy solicitor, a finance broker experienced in bridging and development loans, a RICS surveyor, a structural engineer, a planning consultant, a quantity surveyor, and an accountant. Commercial conversion is a team sport having the right experts in place from day one protects you from costly mistakes and accelerates your progress.

c. Start Analyzing Deals Weekly

Consistency is everything. Review commercial listings every week and run quick feasibility checks. Focus on the fundamentals of commercial conversion: purchase price, build cost, uplift potential, rental demand, and refinance viability. Look for buildings that qualify under Class MA, have good natural light, and offer efficient layouts. The more deals you analyze, the sharper your instincts become.

d. Walk Buildings in Person

Online research is useful, but nothing replaces stepping inside a building. Aim to view at least five to ten commercial properties per month. Walking the space helps you understand ceiling heights, structural layout, access points, and natural light all critical factors in conversion. These visits build confidence and help you spot opportunities others overlook.

e. Make Offers Consistently

Commercial sellers expect negotiation. Make offers based on numbers, not emotion. Use your feasibility calculations to determine your maximum purchase price, then submit offers confidently and consistently. Many deals are won simply because the investor showed up, followed up, and stayed professional throughout the process.

f. Plan Your First Conversion

Once you secure a building, work with your contractor and QS to create a detailed scope of work, timeline, and budget. Identify structural changes, fire safety requirements, insulation upgrades, and layout improvements. A clear plan reduces delays, controls costs, and ensures your project meets building regulations and lender expectations.

g. Refinance and Repeat

After completing the conversion, refinance the property based on its new residential value. This allows you to recycle your capital and move on to the next project. Over time, this cycle acquires, convert, refinance, repeat becomes a powerful engine for portfolio growth and long-term wealth creation.

h. Protect Your Wealth

As your portfolio grows, structure becomes essential. Work with your accountant to ensure your company setup, tax planning, and record-recordkeeping support your long-term goals. Track expenses, maintain compliance documents, and plan for inheritance and succession. Wealth is not just created it is protected through discipline and structure.

15-Minute Commercial Property Viewing Checklist

A fast, focused inspection guide for commercial-to-residential investors

Exterior (2 Minutes)

A commercial building's exterior reveals more about its condition than any agent will tell you. Start with the roof look for missing tiles, sagging sections, damaged flashing, or chimney deterioration. Move to gutters and downpipes; leaks, cracks, and blockages often signal long-term neglect. Inspect brickwork for cracks, damp staining, or signs of structural movement. Check windows for rot, blown glazing, or insecure frames. Finally, assess the surroundings: parking availability, access for contractors, and the condition of neighboring properties all influence conversion viability.

Entrance & Ground-Floor Access (2 Minutes)

The entrance sets the tone for the building's overall condition. Begin with the smell test damp, mould, or sewage odors often indicate hidden issues. Check floors for sloping, soft spots, or unevenness, which may suggest structural concerns. Inspect the electrics: note the age of the consumer unit, exposed wiring, or outdated fittings. Look at ceilings for cracks, stains, or evidence of leaks from upper floors or roof spaces. These early signs help you decide whether the building is worth deeper investigation.

Former Commercial Areas / Open-Plan Spaces (2 Minutes)

Commercial units often have large open areas that will become future living spaces. Inspect walls for damp patches, bubbling paint, or cracks that may indicate water ingress or structural stress. Test windows for functionality, condensation, and security. Check the heating system radiators, pipework, and boiler location to understand upgrade requirements. Assess the layout for reconfiguration potential: can you create natural-light-compliant rooms, protected escape routes, and efficient circulation?

Kitchen or Staff Room Areas (2 Minutes)

Many commercial buildings have outdated staff kitchens or break rooms. Test water pressure at taps. Look under the sink for leaks, mould, or deteriorated pipework. Check flooring for movement, rot, or damage. Assess whether the space can be modernized or repurposed into a compliant residential kitchen. These areas often require full replacement, so note the cost implications.

Bathrooms or WC Areas (2 Minutes)

Commercial WCs vary widely in condition. Test water pressure at taps and showers if present. Check ventilation either an extractor fan or an operable window is essential. Look for leaks, mould, or staining around toilets, sinks, and tiles. Test toilet stability; movement can indicate subfloor issues. These rooms often reveal the building's plumbing health.

Upper Floors / Bedrooms (2 Minutes)

If the building has upper floors or former office rooms, inspect for damp in corners, behind furniture, and around cold spots. Check windows for condition and natural light crucial for residential compliance. Look for cracks and determine whether they appear structural or cosmetic. These floors often convert most easily, so ensure they are structurally sound.

Loft & Final Compliance Checks (1 Minute)

If accessible, inspect the loft for insulation levels, water tanks, and visible roof structure. Check the boiler's age and service history replacement may be required for EPC compliance. Review the EPC rating and potential improvements. These final checks help you estimate upgrade costs and energy-efficiency requirements.

Use Classes Made Simple (For Beginners)

The UK planning system groups buildings into "use classes." Each class tells you what a building is allowed to be used for.

Here is the simplified version:
Class E; Commercial (The Big One)
What it means: Shops, offices, cafés, gyms, nurseries, clinics, light industrial.
Used for: Most modern commercial buildings.
Why it matters: You can convert many Class E buildings into homes (C3) using Class MA permitted development.

Class C; Residential & Living Uses
C1; Hotels
Hotels, guest houses.
C2; Residential Institutions
Care homes, hospitals, boarding schools.
C2A; Secure Institutions
Prisons, secure hospitals.
C3; Homes
Houses, flats, apartments.

This is the class you convert INTO.
C4; Small HMOs
3–6 unrelated people sharing.

Class B; Industrial & Storage

B2; Industrial

Factories, manufacturing.
B8; Storage & Distribution
Warehouses, storage units.

Class F; Community & Learning

F1; Learning & Institutions
Schools, libraries, museums, churches.
F2; Local Community Uses
Small local shops, community halls, sports areas.

Sui Generis: "In Its Own Category"

Used for things that don't fit anywhere else.

Examples:

- Takeaways
- Pubs
- Nightclubs
- Large HMOs (7+ people)
- Petrol stations
- Casinos
- Theatres
- Tattoo studios

Usually requires full planning to change.

Author's Note

When I first stepped into the world of commercial property conversion, I quickly realized something: the buildings weren't the real challenge the mindset was. Empty shops, tired offices, forgotten pubs… they all had stories, potential, and hidden value. But most people walked past them without a second thought. They saw decline. I saw opportunity.

This book was written to help you develop that same lens the ability to look at a building and imagine what it could be, not what it currently is. Commercial conversion is not simply a strategy; it is a way of thinking. It rewards creativity, discipline, and courage. It demands that you learn the rules, respect the process, and surround yourself with the right people. But above all, it invites you to participate in something bigger than profit: the regeneration of communities, the creation of homes, and the transformation of neglected spaces into places where people can live, grow, and thrive.

If you've made it to this point in the book, you already have something many investors never develop the willingness to learn deeply, think strategically, and take responsibility for your own growth. That alone sets you apart. My hope is that the frameworks, checklists, case studies, and roadmaps you've read here become tools you return to again and again. Not because you need reassurance, but because you are building a system a repeatable, scalable approach to commercial conversion that will serve you for years to come.

Thank you for allowing me to guide you through this journey. I wrote this book to empower you, the investor, the creator, the problem-solver to step confidently into a space that is full of opportunity for those who understand it.

Obinna

Disclaimer

This book is for educational and general information purposes only. It is designed to help readers understand the principles, processes, and considerations involved in commercial-to-residential property conversion in the United Kingdom. While every effort has been made to ensure accuracy at the time of writing, property law, planning policy, finance products, tax rules, and building regulations can change. Readers should always verify current requirements and seek professional advice before acting on any information contained in this book.

Nothing in this book constitutes legal advice, financial advice, tax advice, investment advice, or professional guidance specific to any individual situation. Every property, every deal, and every investor's circumstances are different. Decisions should be made only after consulting qualified professionals such as solicitors, planning consultants, surveyors, accountants, tax advisors, and regulated financial specialists.

The examples, case studies, and scenarios included in this book are illustrative only. They are not guarantees of results, nor do they represent typical outcomes. Property investment carries risks, including financial loss, planning refusal, construction challenges, market fluctuations, and compliance obligations. Readers are responsible for conducting their own due diligence and assessing their own risk tolerance.

The author and publisher accept no liability for any loss, damage, or consequences arising from reliance on the information provided. By reading this book, you acknowledge that you are solely responsible for your own decisions and actions.

Commercial conversion can be a powerful strategy but like all investment activities, it requires care, competence, and professional support. Use this book as a guide, not a substitute for expert advice.

www.ingramcontent.com/pod-product-compliance
Lightning Source LLC
LaVergne TN
LVHW070247220926
848482LV00034B/440
* 9 7 8 1 9 1 8 6 5 7 3 2 6 *